INTRODUCTION TO

The Study of Law

S.M. Waddams

M.A., LL.B., LL.M., S.J.D.
PROFESSOR OF LAW
UNIVERSITY OF TORONTO

Fourth Edition

CARSWELL
Thomson Professional Publishing

Canadian Cataloguing in Publication Data

Waddams, S.M., 1942—
Introduction to the study of law

4th ed.
Includes index.
ISBN 0-459-55134-5 (bound) ISBN 0-459-55136-1 (pbk.)

1. Law — Canada. 2. Legal research — Canada.
3. Law — Canada — Study and teaching (Higher).
I. Title.

KE444.W344 1992 349.71 C92-094285-7

Typesetting: Video Text Inc., Barrie, Ontario, Canada

CARSWELL
Thomson Professional Publishing

One Corporate Plaza, 2075 Kennedy Road, Scarborough, Ontario M1T 3V4
Customer Service:
Toronto 1-416-609-3800
Elsewhere in Canada/U.S. 1-800-387-5164
Fax 1-800-298-5094

Lord, what love have I unto thy law; all
the day long is my study in it.

Psalm cxix, 97

FOREWORD

The publication of this "little book" must bring joy to the heart of anyone interested in legal education in Canada. It fills a long-standing need. Until now, the student contemplating the study of law or, having made the decision, beginning his or her never-to-be-forgotten experience, has been filled with apprehension. Most students in either of these two categories do not, today, come from backgrounds that would give them a good idea of what law, and particularly the study of law, is all about. There is, then, the mystery, if not the fear, of the unfamiliar. Not a few of them entertain doubts about their decision, arising, perhaps, out of a feeling of guilt for having abandoned their undergraduate field of study for a discipline leading to the practice of a profession. "What justification," they may ask themselves, "is there for a professional course in a university?" That question, astonishingly enough, continues to be asked, despite the historic association of the study of law and universities of the world. It is a question which this book should help put to rest. Finally, for our puzzled student, there is the inevitable confusion, and frequently accompanying insecurity, associated with a new way of examining, analyzing and solving difficult intellectual questions affecting the relationships of real human beings in an increasingly complex society.

Professor Waddams tells us that the principal architect of modern Canadian legal education, Dean C.A. Wright, described the study of law as "high adventure". Non-lawyers might be forgiven for wondering how objective that brilliant scholar and teacher could have been about a subject to which he had devoted his life. But high adventure is indeed what studying law is, and no reader can come away from this book without sensing the adventure that awaits him or her. The author not only tells his audience how exciting legal analysis is but, in exceptional simplicity, demonstrates it by his very manner of telling. Along the way he strips away the confusion and mystery commonly and, it must be admitted, justifiably, associated with many of our Canadian legal institutions.

Perhaps most characteristic of law as an intellectual subject is its concern with the precision of language. To me the chief virtue of this introduction to the study of law is the example shown in the economy and precision of the words chosen by the author to demonstrate the points he makes. Clear thinking requires clarity of communication. Dean Wright's career may, in the eyes of many, raise a suspicion of bias. Two men of letters he was fond of turning to for support may be more acceptable. In *The House of Intellect*, Jacques Barzun, in his chapter on the language of learning and pedantry wrote:

> . . .contempt and ingratitude toward the interpreters of law is a grave fault. It shows ignorance of the long, arduous growth and superior merit of an institution to which we owe our ease and privileges as thinking beings. The law is a model of intellectual work, and it is a work of words. It is a profession easy to ridicule by its externals and it is criticizable, like other institutions, for its anachronisms. But as an attempt of the *esprit de finesse* to mold coherent conceptions of the true and the just on the restless multiplicity of human life, it is a triumph of articulateness and exactitude. . . .

The American poet, Archibald MacLeish, speaking of his experience with the Socratic method, described by Professor Waddams, said:

> My education such as it is, began . . . in the [Harvard Law] School. I say this not because the occasion demands it (I have said it often and elsewhere), but because it is true. And what was the substance of that education? The Socratic spark which set insatiable fires where no flame was ever seen before. . . . But beyond the spark? Beyond the spark a vision — the vision of the human mind, the great tradition of the intellectual past which knows the bearings of the future. No one, not the most erudite or scholarly man, who has failed to see that vision can truly serve the art of poetry or any other art, and by no study better than the study of the law can that great sight be seen. The law has one way of seeing it. Poetry has another. But the journey is the same.

The full sight can be had only as the student progresses but, this book will, I am confident, provide a glimpse. I do not know anyone else who could have written it. If one detects an abundance of enthusiasm in what I have written, this foreword has served its purpose. Only a few of the readers of this work can expect to have its author as a teacher. By reading his words all others, alas, will have to settle for the next best thing.

Horace Krever

PREFACE

This little book is written for students beginning or seriously contemplating the study of law in the common law provinces of Canada. It is neither a textbook nor a scholarly treatise. Its aim is to bring home to the reader some of the ideas about law that must be grasped by the student. It is not a book on the Canadian legal system, as such, but it attempts to give the reader enough knowledge about the structure of the legal system in Canada and enough of the ideas of law that are common currency in the professional and academic legal world to enable the student to approach legal studies with greater knowledge and, it is hoped, enjoyment than there might otherwise be. For the student who is considering, but has not yet embarked on, a course of legal studies, it is hoped that the book will impart some ideas worth thinking about and something of the flavour of the law.

In writing this book I have drawn from many sources. I am indebted to my own teachers, to my students, and to my colleagues, particularly to Professors Alexander, Prichard and Sharpe who made very helpful suggestions. Among written sources I am indebted particularly to my own introduction to the study of law, Professor Williams' *Learning the Law* and to Sir Robert Megarry's superb collections of legal memorabilia, *Miscellany-at-Law* and *A Second Miscellany-at-Law*.

In the course of the book I have touched rather lightly on difficult and complex matters. Where opinions differ on any question, I have tried to indicate the main outlines of the opposing views, not, of course, because I think that a complex question can be disposed of in a few sentences, but in order to convey to the reader some of the interest and intellectual excitement that attends the study of law. The late C.A. Wright was exaggerating only slightly when, as Dean of the University of Toronto law school, he used to tell the incoming students that the study of law was "high adventure".

Toronto   S.M. Waddams

PREFACE

TABLE OF CONTENTS

TABLE OF CASES

1

WHAT IS LAW?

INTRODUCTION

A question like that in the title to this chapter is not to be answered in a few words, or even in a few books. Indeed, those responding to the question, even lawyers, will always differ from each other in their answers, because the concept of law is so basic to our ideas of society that it has no clear meaning outside the writer's own social and political philosophy. No doubt Canadian law is one thing to a capitalist, and quite another to a Marxist. Further, pre-revolutionary law in a Marxist state is one thing. Post-revolutionary law is something quite different.

Aristotle said that the human person is a political animal. He did not, of course, have in mind the party politics of the twentieth century. He meant that human beings naturally live in a community (the polis or city-state being the particular kind of community he had in mind).[1] This view remains generally accepted. Despite the emphasis we place on the person as an individual, it can hardly be doubted that it is part of her nature to live in a community. As a modern commentator said, the human being is not purely a social animal, nor a solitary animal, he is a social and a solitary animal at the same time.[2] No complete description of humanity could possibly avoid reference to the community as well as to the individual.

A universal feature of human society has been conflict. Individuals have individual interests. On occasion, they conflict with each other. If a society is to survive it must develop a system of resolving conflicts

---

1 Aristotle, *Politics*, i, 2, 9. 1253a (Newman ed.).
2 J. Bronowski, *The Ascent of Man* (1973), p. 411. "Justice is a universal of all cultures. It is a tightrope that man walks between his desire to fulfil his wishes, and his acknowledgement of social responsibility. No animal is faced with this dilemma: an animal is either social or solitary. Man alone aspires to be both, a social solitary."

between individuals, and conflicts between individuals on the one hand and the community on the other. On the other hand, societies share certain values in common. The law manifests the common values of a society, and, at the same time, supplies a system for resolving its conflicts.

SOCIAL SCIENCE OR HUMANITY?

Thus, the law in any society is the society's attempt to resolve the most basic of human tensions, that between the needs of the person as an individual, and her needs as a member of a community. The law is the knife-edge on which the delicate balance is maintained between the individual on the one hand and the society on the other.

Law is, therefore, at the same time, a social science and a humanity. Indeed, it is fundamental to both, and constitutes the bridge between them. Until recently the study of law in most Canadian universities has been rather isolated both from the Social Sciences and the Humanities. In most universities the Faculty of Law is independent of the Faculty of Arts and Science. The Humanities and Social Sciences research libraries rarely include collections of law books. In the last few years, however, much greater interest has been shown in the law faculties, and in other divisions of the universities, in exploring the relationship between law and other academic disciplines.

ACADEMIC STUDY OR PRACTICAL TRAINING?

Part of the reason for the isolation of the law in the university undoubtedly lies in the pragmatic nature of legal study. One can talk at considerable length about the reconciliation of the individual and the community, but the study of law brings the lawyer down very suddenly from the purity of theoretical speculation to the sordid reality of practical needs. Can the police compel a suspected bank robber to undergo surgery against his will in order to discover whether a foreign body lodged in his shoulder is a bullet? Well, on the one hand, the interests of the community require us to facilitate police investigations, and it would be very useful for the police to discover whether the object is a bullet. The safety of society requires an effective police and reasonable regularity in punishment of the guilty. But then, on the other hand, there is the sanctity of the human person, which every free society must respect. We cannot allow the police to cut people up to look at their insides even if it would make their job easier. Yes, but can we do it (the police will ask)? The police surgeon is free at four this afternoon. Can I stop them (the prisoner will ask you)? And how? And quickly? These are the questions that will be asked of lawyers and judges, and they demand answers. Mr. Justice Hugessen of the Quebec Court of Queen's Bench had to give one on July 7, 1972.[3]

Sometimes people are heard to advocate the study of law as a "liberal art", thereby implying that inquiry into what the law actually is can be eliminated and that the existing law schools should reform themselves or take their crass pragmatism elsewhere. The study of law, however, can never divorce itself from a living working system. A theoretical study of police powers without attention to what the police can actually do in a particular society is not a study of law. The bridge between the theoretical and the practical is of the essence. This is not to suggest that there is no place outside the law schools for the study of law. It will be suggested below what approach such study should take.

RULES OR PROCESS?

Many think of the law as a set of rules, and, in part, it is. The law does regulate conduct. However, the study of law is not the learning of rules. Perhaps the biggest surprise to a beginning law student is to discover the uncertainty of legal answers even to basic questions. I should rather say, especially to basic questions, for the more basic the question the greater the uncertainty. Definite answers can often be given to trivial questions: Is income tax payable on an employee's bonus? Is it an offence to sell securities without a licence? It is the fundamental questions that prove elusive: is a person guilty of crime when compelled by necessity to do the forbidden act? Can damages be awarded for loss caused by a breach of contract, even though the loss could not reasonably have been anticipated? These questions raise fundamental issues about the nature and purpose of criminal law and punishment and of contract law and damages. They are not to be easily answered. It is questions of the latter type that mainly concern university law students. It has often been pointed out that the problems studied in law school do not reflect the experience of most lawyers in practice. The law schools make no apology for this. It would be absurd to suggest that a legal education should mirror the experience of practising lawyers. Most lawyers spend their time in executing routine transactions, and avoiding like the plague any problem of complexity or theoretical interest. A busy lawyer does not have time for such luxuries. But a law school goes out of its way to pick out the unusual and interesting case — the case that is on the edge of a legal principle — the case that causes conflict between two different principles.

---

3 *Re Laporte and The Queen* (1972), 8 C.C.C. (2d) 343 (Que. Q.B.).

A very well known case in criminal law is *The Queen v. Dudley and Stephens.*[4] The facts were dramatic. Three men and a boy were cast adrift on the open sea a thousand miles from land. Threatened with starvation, two of them killed and ate the boy. The existence of the report makes it unnecesary to add that they survived to face trial. Plainly the case raises many complex issues, legal and ethical, and is well worth some time in any curriculum. However, it can safely be predicted that not one in a million law graduates will run across a similar case in practice. The law schools do not apologize for emphasizing unusual cases; they go out of their way to look for them. *Dudley and Stephens* is one of the few cases on the defence of necessity in criminal law; and what other cases there are show that the law is in a state of great uncertainty. Even in more mundane areas, the law is full of uncertainty, and quite rapid change. Until quite recently most Canadian lawyers thought that a party complaining of breach of contract was not entitled to damages for mental distress, disappointment, anger or frustration. In 1972, a court held a holiday tour operator liable for such damages to a customer whose holiday failed to match the expectations engendered by the defendant's glossy brochures.[5] What is the law after that case? Does the principle extend to the seller of a defective motor home, or to an employer who wrongly dismisses an employee, or to a solicitor who fails to provide proper legal services? No one can say until the courts decide. There are tenable arguments for and against extending the principle of liability to each of the classes of persons mentioned. As each decision is reported, the law changes, and it is still quite uncertain. It is much closer to the truth to regard the law as a continuing process of attempting to solve the problems of a changing society, than as a set of rules.

It has been said that everyone is presumed to know the law, but this is a fiction to support the rule that ignorance of the criminal law is no excuse. Plainly everyone does not know the law. Indeed, another rule, that a misrepresentation of law is of no legal consequence, has been justified on the basis that the law is so uncertain that any statement of law is equivalent only to an expression of an opinion! An eighteenth century judge pointed out that "it would be very hard upon the profession, if the law was so certain, that every body knew it,"[6] and another judge is reputed to have said that everyone is presumed to know the law except Her Majesty's judges, who have a Court of Appeal set over them to correct their errors.

---

4 (1884), 14 Q.B.D. 273.

5 *Jarvis v. Swans Tours Ltd.*, [1973] 1 Q.B. 233 (C.A.).

6 *Jones v. Randall* (1774), 1 Cowp. 37 at 40.

THE IDEA OF JUSTICE

Everyone knows that the law is not the same thing as justice. Generally, indeed, when the two words are mentioned in the same sentence, it is by way of contrast. It is rare that a resolution of a dispute leaves both parties equally happy, and it would be Utopian to expect that a working system should satisfy the losing party all the time. The best that can be expected is that the losing party will admit that she has had a fair hearing according to fair procedures and that the result has been determined by principles that she will recognize as the appropriate sort of principles to apply in such a case.

It is a well known aphorism that hard cases make bad law— that is, sympathy for a party in a particular case may lead the court to distort a legal principle in order to secure a successful result for that party. There is a perpetual tension in the law between stability, certainty and predictability on the one hand, and equity, fairness and justice in the individual case on the other. An advocate of the former set of values spoke disparagingly of that "vague jurisprudence which is sometimes attractively styled justice as between man and man," which he then proceeded to dismiss as "well-meaning sloppiness of thought."[7] A later judge said that he would not be drawn by some abstract idea of justice to ignore his first duty, which was to administer the law.[8] Yet, despite heavy emphasis, particularly in the nineteenth and early twentieth centuries, on stable and predictable rules, a study of the actual decisions of judges shows that they will attempt to evade rules that seem to produce unfair results.

Justice is an elusive word. It commonly means "that point of view on a particular issue that I hold myself", as in "justice for the workers" or "let us fight for justice". Sometimes it is deliberately meaningless, as when the clergy pray for peace with justice in southern Africa, or a just settlement to the transit strike. The lawyer's concept of justice is much closer to the concept of rationality. If disputes are determined by fair procedures before an impartial tribunal honestly trying to give rational and consistent reasons for its results, we will not satisfy every litigant all the time, but we will come as close as humanly possible to administering justice. Professor John Willis, a distinguished Canadian law teacher, said that the law is a part of Western society's dream of a life governed by reason.

It is commonly thought that any dispute has a "right" or "just" result, and if only sufficient effort and goodwill is spent, that result can be found.

---

7 *Holt v. Markham*, [1923] 1 K.B. 504 at 513 (C.A.) *per* Scrutton L.J.

8 *Scruttons Ltd. v. Midland Silicones Ltd.*, [1962] A.C. 446 at 467-8 (H.L.) *per* Viscount Simonds.

But even a brief introduction to legal problems shows the weakness of this view. Consider the case of sale by a non-owner to a good-faith buyer. B steals A's watch and sells it to C, who pays value for it in good faith. Everyone can agree that justice requires B to repay. But what if B is not available, as is common in such cases, having disappeared, or is found without assets? It is not at all obvious what result "justice" requires in solving the dispute between A and C. A will assert: "This is my watch; give it back. If you were so foolish or unfortunate as to pay money to a rogue for something that he had no right to sell, so much the worse for you." C will say: "I have paid good money for this watch. I bought it in good faith, and if you had not left it lying around to be stolen, the problem would never have arisen. Further, you probably have insurance against loss by theft (or you should have). I am not insured against loss by law suit of my purchase." There is something in all of these points. No obvious solution leaps to the eye. In resolving a dispute of this sort, the court must have an eye not only to justice between the parties to the particular dispute, but to the long-term effects that the decision may have. Suppose the law is established in favour of C, the good faith buyer. Might this encourage theft? It would mean that thieves could pass a good title to buyers — admittedly, only to good-faith buyers, but bad faith is always hard to prove, and the buyer might be a little less inclined to be suspicious of a good bargain if he knew that the law would generally give him a good title. Further, is it wise to recognize theft as an effective way of transferring title? Is there not a value in "stability of ownership"? On the other hand, if the law is established in A's favour, might it make owners careless in looking after their goods? Will it affect freedom of commerce if no buyer can be sure that she is getting good title? Is there a value in "stability of transactions"? No obvious answer appears and, indeed, there can be no final resolution to the tension between stability of ownership and stability of transactions. Both are values that the law must recognize and protect. The difficult and interesting cases are those that bring the two principles into sharp conflict, and compel a choice. It is the attempt to make that choice rationally and consistently that we can reasonably call the administration of justice.

THE RULE OF LAW

This is another elusive phrase that is apt to be used in support of many different arguments. In one sense it describes an ordered society as opposed to one where the person with the gun always gets his own way. It conjures up the vision of stability and tranquility that the framers of Canadian confederation had in mind when they spoke of the "Peace,

Order, and good Government of Canada."[9] A similar view underlies the mottos: "Freedom under the law", and "Equal justice under law".

The rule of law suggests judicial independence of the executive branch of government. It was established in the seventeenth century by Chief Justice Coke that even the King could not interfere with the ordinary processes of justice.[10] In the United States the Watergate crisis in 1974 reaffirmed the principle in holding that the President was bound to obey the court. In Canada in 1945, a government agency asserted the power under wartime emergency regulations to prevent the carrying out of an order of the court. Wilson J.'s response was in the following very fine language:

> If I have been unable to find an exact precedent for my decision in this matter, it is not, I hope, through lack of diligence but because the action attempted by the administrator is unprecedented. This is, so far as I know, the first instance in the annals of British jurisprudence in which an official has essayed to invalidate the order of a Court of Justice. It is, I think, somewhat alarming to find an official of a minor administrative bureau attempting to assert a power which was, so long ago as the reign of James I, denied to the King himself. I refer, of course, to the glorious and courageous refusal of Coke and his brother Judges of the Court of King's Bench to obey the King's writ *de non procedendo rege inconsulto* [not to proceed without consulting the King] commanding them to stop or delay proceedings in their Court. . . . The whole value of the legal system — the integrity of the rule of law — is at once destroyed if it becomes possible for officials by arbitrary decisions made, not in the public court rooms but in the private offices of officialdom, without hearing the parties, without taking evidence, free of all obedience to settled legal principles, and subject to no appeal, effectively to overrule the Courts and deprive a Canadian citizen of a right he has established by the immemorial method of a trial at law.[11]

In the modern parliamentary system where the government often controls the majority of the Legislature, we are sometimes apt to confuse the government with Parliament itself. But it still remains an essential principle of our constitution that the government cannot itself make law, and has only those powers given to it by law. It is certainly not less important now than formerly for the courts to assert their ancient power of ensuring that officials of government at all levels do respect and obey the law.

The rule of law is also used to describe an ideal of rationality in the ordering of society, as opposed to the arbitrary making of decisions. It is often said that we should be governed by laws, not by the whims of persons. The concept is closely linked with the idea of justice described in the last section. We will be governed not necessarily by decisions that

---

9 Constitution Act, 1867 (U.K.), c. 3, s. 91.
10 See *Colt v. Coventry & Lichfield* (1617), 1 Roll Rep. 451.
11 *Re Bachand and Dupuis*, [1946] 2 D.L.R. 641 at 654-5 (B.C.S.C.).

we would like, but by decisions made by impartial persons applying settled, consistent and rationally defensible general principles.

The two meanings of the phrase sometimes conflict quite starkly. When a government is threatened by civil insurrection it may well announce that it proposes to restore the rule of law. Quite often it will do so by suspending the ordinary democratic processes and infringing the ordinary civil liberties of its citizens, that is, by suspending the rule of law in the second sense. Of course, the government will generally claim that in such circumstances the democratic processes and civil liberties are suspended only temporarily in order to ensure their long-term survival. Sometimes, but not always, history bears out that claim.

Another aspect of the rule of law is the avoidance of retroactive decision-making. Particularly in criminal law it is thought to be of importance that conduct lawful when engaged in should not retroactively be made punishable. This is called the principle of legality often expressed in the Latin phrase *"nulla poena sine lege"* — no punishment without a law. A civil judicial decision that departs sharply from prior law is by its nature retroactive in its effect on the parties to a dispute, and this is one reason for judicial caution in law-making. In interpreting statutes the judges, for similar reasons, always lean in favour of finding that statutes are not retroactive in effect, that they do not make punishable conduct that was lawful at the time, and do not take away vested rights without compensation.

The rule of law has been attacked by some on political grounds; it has been suggested that the concept is a myth that conceals the reality of class power. Of this kind of claim, the historian, E.P. Thompson, has written, on the basis of a study of eighteenth century English criminal law:

> I am insisting ... upon the obvious point, which some modern theorists have overlooked, that there is a difference between arbitrary power and the rule of law. We ought to expose the shams and inequities which may be concealed beneath this law. But the rule of law itself, the imposing of effective inhibitions upon power and the defence of the citizen from power's all-intrusive claims, seems to me to be an unqualified human good. ... I am told that, just beyond the horizon, new forms of working-class power are about to arise which, being founded upon egalitarian productive relations, will require no inhibition and can dispense with the negative restrictions of bourgeois legalism. A historian is unqualified to pronounce on such Utopian projections. All that he knows is that he can bring in support of them no historical evidence whatsoever. His advice might be: watch this new power for a century or two before you cut your hedges down.[12]

---

12 E.P. Thompson, *Whigs and Hunters* (Penguin, 1977), p. 266.

THE ROLE OF THE JUDGES

The idea of justice and the rule of law are both ideals — part of Western society's dream — never fully attainable. So is the concept of the impartial tribunal. No judge can free herself from her background and surroundings. In a sense no judge who is not an automaton can be completely impartial. But we consider the ideal of sufficient value to attempt the creation of tribunals that are as impartial as humanly possible. This is the justification for the security of tenure given to judges and for the elevated status we attempt to give them by the design of courtrooms, by the dress worn in court by judges and counsel, by the respectful and archaic forms of address used to judges in and out of court. We do not really think that the judge personally is worthy of veneration when we address him or her as "My Lord" or "My Lady". It is all part of an attempt to preserve, so far as we can, the real and apparent impartiality of the judge. It is easier to perceive the judge as impartial if he is seen not just as an old pal whom you might call on the telephone for a chat about tomorrow's case, but as a minister of justice. Isolation of the judge and formalization of his office helps not only the public perception of his role, but it assists the judge's perception of his own role.

It is often suggested that we could dispense with legal argument and simply ask the judge to make a sensible decision. This concept of decision-making is sometimes (critically) called "palm tree justice", the image being of a wise person sitting in the shade under a palm tree dispensing the wisdom of Solomon to all comers.[13]

The objection to such a system is based on the concept of a rational system of justice mentioned above. It is a short step from the wise decision without reasons to the arbitrary decision. "The discretion of a judge is the law of tyrants."[14] There is no better guarantee of impartiality and rationality in decision-making than the requirement of reasons open to the scrutiny of the public and of an appellate tribunal. Procedure and substance are intertwined. If we set up a system where rational decisions are not formally required, we will not get rational decisions.

A fundamental concept of our legal system is that like cases should be decided alike, that is, that there must be justice as between plaintiff and plaintiff and as between defendant and defendant, as well as between

---

13 Speaking of emergency wartime legislation Goddard L.J. said in *Metropolitan Properties Co. v. Purdy*, [1940] 1 All E.R. 188 at 191 (C.A.): "the court . . . is really put very much in the position of a Cadi under the palm tree. There are no principles on which he is directed to act. He has to do the best he can in the circumstances, having no rules of law to guide him . . .

14 *Doe d. Hindson v. Kersey* (1765) *per* Lord Camden C.J., quoted in Megarry, *Miscellany-at-Law* (1955), p. 219.

plaintiff and defendant. Consider the case outlined above of the thief who sells to a good-faith buyer. A decision for the owner might be "just" in case 1. A decision for the buyer in identical case 2 might arguably also be "just" as between the parties, but it would not be just as between the owner in the first case and the owner in the second. The court in the second case therefore feels immense pressure to explain the difference between the cases if it is to justify a different result. From this pressure springs the doctrine of precedent, or *stare decisis* (standing by former decisions).

An American judge said:

> It is sometimes said that this adherence to precedent is slavish; that it fetters the mind of the judge, and compels him to decide without reference to principle. But let it be remembered that *stare decisis* is itself a principle of great magnitude and importance. It is absolutely necessary to the formation and permanence of any system of jurisprudence. Without it we may fairly be said to have no law; for law is a fixed and established *rule*, not depending in the slightest degree on the caprice of those who may happen to administer it. . . . The uncertainty of the law — an uncertainty inseparable from the nature of the science — is a great evil at best, and we would aggravate it terribly if we could be blown about by every wind of doctrine, holding for true today what we repudiate as false tomorrow.[15]

There are always distinctions between cases. If arguably rationally significant, case 1 can be "distinguished". It would not be rational to distinguish the cases on the basis of the colour of the owner's hair in each, but it might arguably be relevant that the owner in case 1 was careful to put his watch in a safe place, whereas the owner in case 2 left it lying on a table in a restaurant. Or, of course, case 1 might be wrongly decided (in the opinion of the judge in case 2). But the judge will feel the need to explain why the results are different.

Once the principle is accepted that like cases should be decided alike there is really no escape from the whole paraphernalia of the common law — reports of past cases, reasoned argument, reasons for decision, and appeal and further reasons, not to mention academic commentary on the reasons afterwards. More will be said in later chapters about precedent and the use of decided cases.

Canadian judges in the past have perceived their role as interpreters of the law and as adjudicators, rather than as law-makers in the primary sense. As will be shown in a later chapter,[16] American judges have taken a more activist view of their functions and the enactment of the Canadian Charter of Rights and Freedoms, in 1982, has brought Canadian judges closer to the American view. The alternative views of a judge's proper

---

15 *McDowell v. Oyer*, 21 Pa. Sup. 417 at 423 (1853) *per* Black C.J., quoted in Megarry, *Miscellany-at-Law* (1955), p. 331.
16 Chapter 9, below.

role were sharply brought into focus by a case in the Supreme Court of Canada, *Harrison v. Carswell.*[17]

Ms. Carswell was involved in a labour dispute with her employer whose store was in a shopping plaza. Carswell picketed the store in the usual way by demonstrating in front of it. The owner of the plaza told Carswell that picketing was not allowed in the plaza and that she could only picket on the public sidewalk some distance away. Carswell refused to leave and was convicted under The Manitoba Petty Trespasses Act of trespassing on private property. The question for the Supreme Court of Canada was the propriety of this conviction.

Carswell's position was that there was a general right to picket peacefully in furtherance of a labour dispute, that picketing was a valuable and important right of employees and should not be denied to employees employed in a shopping plaza, that the public had general access to the common parts of the plaza, that the employer received the benefit of public access for the purposes of its business and, therefore, that the plaza sidewalk should be treated as though it were public property for the purpose of picketing. This position was supported by three members of the court, including the then Chief Justice of Canada.

The majority of the court, however, rejected these arguments. Dickson J., giving the majority judgment said:

> The submission that this Court should weigh and determine the respective values to society of the right to property and the right to picket raises important and difficult political and socio-economic issues, the resolution of which must, by their very nature, be arbitrary and embody personal economic and social beliefs. It raises also fundamental questions as to the role of this Court under the Canadian constitution. The duty of the Court, as I envisage it, is to proceed in the discharge of its adjudicative function in a reasoned way from principled decision and established concepts. I do not for a moment doubt the power of the Court to act creatively — it has done so on countless occasions; but manifestly one must ask — what are the limits of the judicial function? There are many and varied answers to this question. Holmes J. said in *Southern Pacific Co. v. Jensen* (1917), 244 U.S. 205 at p. 221: "I recognize without hesitation that the judges do and must legislate, but they can do it only interstitially; they are confined from molar to molecular actions." Cardozo, *The Nature of the Judicial Process* (1921), p. 141, recognized that the freedom of the judge is not absolute in this expression of his view:
>
> > "This judge, even when he is free, is still not wholly free. He is not to innovate at pleasure. He is not a knight-errant, roaming at will in pursuit of his own ideal of beauty or of goodness. He is to draw his inspiration from consecrated principles."

---

17 [1976] 2 S.C.R. 200.

The former Chief Justice of the Australian High Court, Sir Owen Dixon, in an address delivered at Yale University in September 1955, "Concerning Judicial Method", had this to say:

"But in our Australian High Court we have had as yet no deliberate innovators bent on express change of acknowledged doctrine. It is one thing for a court to seek to extend the application of accepted principles to new cases or to reason from the more fundamental of settled legal principles to new conclusions or to decide that a category is not closed against unforeseen instances which in reason might be subsumed thereunder. It is an entirely different thing for a judge, who is discontented with a result held to flow from a long accepted legal principle, deliberately to abandon the principle in the name of justice or of social necessity or of social convenience. The former accords with the technique of the common law and amounts to no more than an enlightened application of modes of reasoning traditionally respected in the courts. It is a process by the repeated use of which the law is developed, is adapted to new conditions, and is improved in content. The latter means an abrupt and almost arbitrary change."

. . .

Society has long since acknowledged that a public interest is served by permitting union members to bring economic pressure to bear upon their respective employers through peaceful picketing, but the right has been exercisable in some locations and not in others and to the extent that picketing has been permitted on private property the right hitherto has been accorded by statute. For example, s. 87 of the *Labour Code of British Columbia Act,* R.S.B.C. 1979, c. 212, s. 87, provides that no action lies in respect of picketing permitted under the Act for trespass to real property to which a member of the public ordinarily has access.

Anglo-Canadian jurisprudence has traditionally recognized, as a fundamental freedom, the right of the individual to the enjoyment of property and the right not to be deprived thereof, or any interest therein, save by due process of law. The Legislature of Manitoba has declared in *The Petty Trespasses Act* that any person who trespasses upon land, the property of another, upon or through which he has been requested by the owner not to enter, is guilty of an offence. If there is to be any change in this statute law, if A is to be given the right to enter and remain on the land of B against the will of B, it would seem to me that such a change must be made by the enacting institution, the Legislature, which is representative of the people and designed to manifest the political will, and not by the Court.[18]

PUBLIC POLICY

Public policy is as elusive a concept as justice itself. Judicial approaches have varied. A nineteenth-century judge said that public policy is an unruly horse and dangerous to ride.[19] A modern English judge said

---

18 *Id.* at 218-19.
19 *Richardson v. Mellish* (1824), 2 Bing. 229 at 252 *per* Burrough J.

of this dictum: "I disagree. With a good man in the saddle, the unruly horse can be kept in control. It can jump over obstacles. It can leap the fences put up by fictions and come down on the side of justice."[20] Even he, however, would not favour arbitrary or whimsical decision-making and would undoubtedly insist on rational principles of horsemanship. Perhaps he would not disagree with an Ontario judge who said: "No Judge has a right to declare that which he does not himself believe in to be against public policy simply because it is against his opinion and his idea of that which is for the welfare of the community."[21]

Judges often say that they propose to ignore policy considerations and simply to apply the law. As law teachers are fond of pointing out, the result is not to avoid a policy decision, but, instead, to apply the perhaps unarticulated policy that underlies the prevailing rule of law. If in a contracts case, for example, it is argued that the agreement is contrary to public policy, the rejection of the argument amounts to a judicial preference for another policy, namely, enforcement of agreements. In one case a person employed to work on a secret radar base in Northern Quebec was prohibited by his contract from "fraternization or association with the native population." From one point of view this provision is racially discriminatory and so surely contrary to one of the strongest public policies in our society. From another point of view, the employee made a perfectly free and fair bargain, no doubt for excellent remuneration, and he should be made to abide by it. The Quebec Courts, affirmed by the Supreme Court of Canada,[22] held that the agreement was enforceable and not contrary to the Quebec equivalent of public policy (public order and good morals). The facts of the case illustrate the elusive nature of public policy, and explain the reluctance of the judges to set themselves up as arbiters of policy. It might seem at first sight that setting aside the obnoxious clause in the agreement would be a great blow struck for racial equality. However, evidence would probably be forthcoming to show that the contractual restrictions were favoured, and possibly instigated, by the leaders of the native communities themselves. Which is the more important policy, equal treatment of all persons regardless of race, or the right of native communities to exclude what they regard as alien influences? Similar dilemmas are raised by the question of free availability to native people of alcohol, and removal of sex discrimination among native people. The right of the individual may be in direct opposition to the wishes of the

---

20 *Enderby Town Football Club Ltd. v. Football Association Ltd.*, [1971] Ch. 591 at 606 *per* Lord Denning M.R.

21 *Re Millar*, [1936] O.R. 554 at 565 (C.A.) *per* Middleton J.A.

22 *Whitfield v. Cdn. Marconi Co.* (1967), 68 D.L.R. (2d) 251 (Que. Q.B.); affirmed (1968), 68 D.L.R. (2d) 766 (S.C.C.).

community. The conflict between individual rights and group rights is one of the most difficult and divisive social issues. The more conservative judges are not entirely to be blamed for keeping a firm hand on the reins of the unruly horse.

The public policy of a community is, of course, determined in many other forums besides the courts. The chief of these is the legislature, and, under the authority of legislation, regulatory boards, tribunals and councils at all levels of government activity.

LAW AND SOCIAL CHANGE

It ought not to require emphasis that the law is not the private preserve of the profession but the mirror of the attitudes of society. This is obviously true of the legislature, which is the chief instrument of law reform. It is not always so clear that the courts, too, reflect the values of a society. Sometimes the courts seem to be out of touch with social attitudes, but there are strong pressures that prevent their getting too far out of touch. An English judge in 1924 said: "An expanding society demands an expanding common law,"[23] and another in 1953 said: "If we never do anything which has not been done before, we shall never get anywhere. The law will stand still whilst the rest of the world goes on; and that will be bad for both."[24] The law cannot lag too far behind, or move too far ahead of, the attitudes of society at large.

A remarkable recent example of law reform by changing social attitudes is the *Morgentaler* case. The Criminal Code prohibited abortion except as approved by a therapeutic abortion committee. Dr. Morgentaler openly performed abortions that had not been so approved. He was prosecuted and acquitted by a jury. On appeal, the Quebec Court of Appeal substituted a conviction and the Supreme Court of Canada upheld the Court of Appeal.[25] The Minister of Justice ordered a new trial and moved to repeal the law that permitted an appellate court to substitute a conviction for a jury acquittal.[26] Dr. Morgentaler was tried a second and a third time and acquitted at both trials.[27] Then the prosecution gave up in Quebec, from which one might conclude that the abortion laws in the Criminal Code, whatever their intrinsic merits, were no longer acceptable to society at large and had become unenforceable. However, Dr. Morgentaler was

---

23 *Prager v. Blatspiel, Stamp & Heacock Ltd.*, [1924] 1 K.B. 566 at 570 *per* McCardie J.
24 *Packer v. Packer*, [1954] P. 15 at 22 *per* Denning L.J.
25 *Morgentaler v. The Queen* (1975), 53 D.L.R. (3d) 161 (S.C.C.).
26 See Criminal Law Amendment Act, 1975 (Can.), c. 93, s. 75 [am. s. 613(4) of the Criminal Code].
27 See *R. v. Morgentaler* (1976), 27 C.C.C. (2d) 81 (Que. C.A.).

subsequently prosecuted in Ontario for performing abortions there. He was again acquitted by a jury, but the Court of Appeal ordered a new trial.[28] On further appeal, the Supreme Court of Canada held that the relevant provision of the Criminal Code was invalid because it conflicted with the Canadian Charter of Rights and Freedoms.[29]

Another instance where the law has responded to a change in social attitudes is in the division of property on the dissolution of marriage. In 1973 the Supreme Court of Canada held that a woman who had helped her husband over many years to build up and maintain a successful ranch was not entitled to any share in the ranch when the marriage broke down.[30] Most people consider this an unjust result and many expressed that view publicly. Five years later on very similar facts the majority of the Supreme Court of Canada held that a wife was entitled to a half-share in her husband's farm, though they were divided in their reasons.[31] Dickson J., speaking for three of the majority of five judges, was acutely conscious of the social implications of the Court's decision and of the Court's duty to administer a kind of justice that reflected the views of contemporary society. His comments on alternative approaches to the judicial function are of general interest. All the judges agreed that if the wife could prove a real intention to share the property, she would win. But in most cases parties to a marriage do not write such things down in black and white; intention is only to be inferred from conduct. Now, if an intention to share property can be inferred from the circumstances of marriage itself and the usual conduct of married people, the effect is very close to laying down a general rule of law that matrimonial property is to be shared. Dickson J. referred to the division of judicial views between those who insisted on finding a real intention to share, and those who were willing to impose a sharing on grounds of justice and equity, irrespective of real intention:

> The settlement of such disputes has been bedevilled by conflicting doctrine and a continuing struggle between the "justice and equity" school . . . and the "intent" school . . . The charge raised against the former school is that of dispensing "palm tree" justice; against the latter school, that of meaningless ritual in searching for a phantom intent . . .
>
> In earlier days the view was taken that on marriage "man and woman are one and that one is the man". The introduction generally of Married Women's Property Acts made it possible for wives to hold separate property but did little otherwise to improve the lot of married women. The custom

---

28 *R. v. Morgentaler* (1985), 52 O.R. (2d) 353 (C.A.).

29 *Morgentaler v. R.*, [1988] 1 S.C.R. 30.

30 *Murdoch v. Murdoch*, [1975] 1 S.C.R. 423.

31 *Rathwell v. Rathwell* (1978), 83 D.L.R. (3d) 289 (S.C.C.).

> by which real estate acquired by a married couple was taken in the name of the husband, coupled with the reverence paid to registered title, militated against wives. . . .
>
> Many factors, legal and non-legal, have emerged to modify the position of earlier days. Among these factors are a more enlightened attitude towards the status of women, altered lifestyles, dynamic socio-economic changes. Increasingly, the work of a woman in the management of the home and rearing of the children, as wife and mother, is recognized as an economic contribution to the family unit.[32]

The very rapid changes in social attitudes is reflected in change in judicial attitudes, like those of Dickson J., and also in family property legislation in a number of jurisdictions, including Saskatchewan where the case just discussed arose.

In 1964 Ontario established a Law Reform Commission, and most of the other provinces and the Government of Canada followed suit in the next few years. The Law Reform Commissions have initiated some very valuable improvements to the law, particularly in areas of no great political interest, where in the absence of a Law Reform Commission the government would be unlikely to intervene (this is, what is sometimes called "Lawyers' Law"). Lawyers' Law cannot, however, be divorced from questions of social policy, and there is still a somewhat uneasy relationship between the quasi-independent Law Reform Commissions and the politically responsible governmental departments. Controversial questions of social policy must ultimately be introduced in the legislature by a politically responsible government. But even on such matters the Law Reform Commissions can play a useful role by initiating and supervising thorough and independent research, by looking at proposed legislation dispassionately, and pointing out anomalies that are likely to arise from particular proposals. If the Commissions do not do so before the legislation is enacted, it is likely that they will be called upon afterwards to patch up the deficiencies in the legislation.

DIVISIONS AND SOURCES OF LAW

Disputes arise between individuals, between an individual and the community, between different governments in a federal state, and between states. The law applicable to disputes between individuals is generally called private law, or (in contradistinction to criminal law) civil law.[33]

---

32 *Id.* at 297-8.

33 "Civil law" varies in meaning according to the context. It may be contrasted (as here) with criminal law, or with ecclesiastical law, or with military law, or with common law (*e.g.*, "Quebec is a civil law jurisdiction, unlike its common law neighbours").

Disputes between an individual and the state are governed by criminal law, administrative law and constitutional law. Disputes between governments within a federal state are the concern of constitutional law; disputes between states fall into the sphere of public international law. More will be said about these divisions in later chapters.

The study of law is, to a large extent, the study of statutes and judicial decisions. The legislature and the courts are the chief sources of law. In a highly regulated state, however, there are thousands of administrative bodies exercising very important regulatory and adjudicative powers. These bodies are dependent on statutes for their powers, and the extent of those powers must ultimately be interpreted by the courts. However, as a practical matter, the direct effect of regulatory tribunals is often of more importance than the direct effect of legislation or of judicial decisions.

2

LEGAL EDUCATION

THE PURPOSE OF LEGAL EDUCATION

Law teachers are used to being shot at from several directions. Colleagues in other university faculties consider them mere technicians. Law students think, on the contrary, that their teachers are insufficiently practical, and the legal profession regards them as a woolly-minded set of individuals out of touch with reality.

There has always been and there will always be a tension in legal education between the practical and the academic. Law teachers, naturally, differ among themselves in the emphasis that they would give to particular aspects of legal education. There is, however, some common ground. Every law teacher will agree that the study of law must involve a pragmatic element. The theoretical study of legal ideas must always be brought into focus in the context of a living working legal system. Abstract ideas must be disciplined by concrete instances. It is not enough to know how human communities might go about resolving a particular problem; we must know how a court in this jurisdiction in fact resolved it yesterday, and what it is likely to do with it tomorrow. So the theorist cannot ignore the practical. "Without the concrete instances the general proposition is baggage, impedimenta, stuff about the feet."[1]

Neither can the practitioner ignore the theory. A seventeenth-century judge said that he knoweth not the law who knoweth not the reason thereof.[2]

---

1 Llewellyn, *The Bramble Bush* (1960 ed.) p. 12.

2 "The reason of the law is the life of the law; for though a man can tell the law, yet if he know not the reason thereof, he shall soon forget his superficial knowledge. But when he findeth the right reason of the law, and so brings it to his natural reason that he comprehendeth it as his own, this will not only serve him for the understanding of that particular case, but of many others . . . and this knowledge will long remain with him." *Coke on Littleton*, Book 3, chapter 3, section 283, p. 183b.

It would, of course, be impossible to learn every single judicial decision as a separate "rule" of law. It would also be fruitless. It is useless to know that on a particular set of facts the law requires a particular result, if the reason for the result is not also appreciated. Without an appreciation of the principle that governs the decision one cannot even begin to pick out from the mass of facts that constitute each case those that are relevant. The good lawyer, and by this I mean the good practising lawyer, as well as the good academic, must appreciate the strengths and weaknesses of the arguments that support each legal "rule". If the arguments are open to challenge, they will be challenged, if not in the lowest courts tomorrow, at least in the Supreme Court of Canada in ten years' time. The well-educated lawyer is equipped to challenge former decisions where they are weak, and to practise law not only in the lower courts tomorrow but to argue either side of the case in the Supreme Court ten years later. The late Professor J.B. Milner, a distinguished Canadian law teacher, said: "We (in the university law schools) aim at giving our students the best possible academic legal education; it just so happens that the best academic education is also the best practical training. Now, isn't that fortunate!"

Professor John Willis made a similar point when in a Convocation Address at York University in 1973 he answered hypothetical but typical student criticisms of law teaching:

> [You complain] that your criminal law teacher spent too much time talking about the limits of the criminal sanction and never got around to doing anything on how to quash an information for duplicity. That your tax teacher seemed to know all about the report of the Carter Commission — "which is now dead as a dodo"— and to have little or no interest in the latest downtown dodge for getting around some of the recent hole-plugging amendments to the Income Tax Act. That your administrative law teacher went on for ages about what kinds of issues were and what were not, in his opinion, suited to decision by the ordinary courts, and was pretty thin on some of the recent Court of Appeal decisions on what is a judicial as opposed to an administrative function in the law of certiorari. Good for those teachers, say I; they got their priorities right. You will have all the rest of your life to track down the very latest learning on duplicity, tax dodges, and certiorari — assuming, and that's quite an assumption, that absurdities such as these will long survive the winds of change that are sweeping through the cobwebbed cloisters of the legal world. What you got from those teachers — some understanding of *real* legal problems, legal problems that are fundamental, legal problems that under new names and new forms will always be with us — will, like the muscular strength of old Father William's jaw, last you the rest of your life.[3]

---

3 June 11, 1973, unpublished.

Most university law teachers would share this philosophy. There is a pleasing paradox in the thought that they give their students the best practical training by refusing to be too practical.

CANADIAN LEGAL EDUCATION

Some light is thrown on the role of the university law school by considering the history of its development. The first and most striking point about the history of Canadian legal education is its brevity. Until the 1940s, with the distinguished exception of Dalhousie Law School, university law schools in their present form did not exist in Canada. Typically, students were prepared for the practice of law by a system of apprenticeship, called articling, with supplementary lectures, mostly by practitioners, organized by the professional governing bodies. In Ontario, in the forties, students attended lectures in the mornings and spent the afternoons in law offices. The University of Toronto did include law in its curriculum, and offered at the time an honours degree in Arts and Law, but since this was not recognized by the Law Society for purposes of admission to practice, comparatively few students took the university degree. In 1949, the late Dr. C.A. Wright, together with other full-time teachers at Osgoode Hall Law School, the Law Society's school, resigned from that school in protest against the Law Society's proposal to reduce the already small academic content of legal education. Wright immediately established a law faculty at the University of Toronto.[4] Subsequently, law faculties on his model were established at four other Ontario universities. In 1967, Osgoode Hall Law School severed its connection with the Law Society and became the law faculty at York University in Toronto.

The pattern of legal education that Wright established at Toronto, and which was copied throughout Canada, was strongly influenced by the American model, in particular Harvard Law School. The curriculum was designed to give students three years of thorough academic grounding in the law. The guiding spirit was a wish to impart a critical understanding of legal institutions, and the scope and purpose of legal rules, rather than simply a training for day-to-day practice. The university did not claim to teach everything the law student would need to know. Many pieces of practical knowledge, it was considered, could best be imparted outside the university, and this duty was left to the profession.

The professional bodies responded to this pattern by instituting a period of practical training, called a Bar Admission Course, to follow the law school curriculum. In most common law provinces this involves a year

---

4 See C.I. Kyer and J.E. Bickenbach, *The Fiercest Debate* (University of Toronto Press, 1987).

of articling with supplementary lectures and seminars. The teaching portion has never been popular with its students, at least during their participation in it. However, the system has often been admired by those less directly connected with it. Professor John Willis, in the Convocation address referred to earlier, said:

> [You should thank] God . . . that you are not, as in some other Provinces, thrust out into the world without knowing "what everyone knows" — everyone, that is to say, but you and your fellow newcomers to the practice of law. For teaching you "what everyone knows" — e.g. how to close a simple estate, how to carry through a simple real estate deal, how many copies of what documents are to be served on whom in civil litigation and so on and so on — is what the deservedly admired Bar Admission Course is trying to do.[5]

Meanwhile the law schools themselves have moved a little from Wright's model towards greater emphasis on the practical. Most law schools have in recent years introduced what are called, by analogy with medical education, "clinical programmes". These programmes aim at fulfilling several different objectives, not all entirely consistent with each other. In part they represent an attempt to include in the university curriculum some of the practical aspects of legal education formerly thought to be more properly the concern of the law societies. In part they attempt to illuminate and enrich the academic curriculum by illustrating the actual current day-to-day application of legal ideas. They are thought to enliven university education by offering a change of milieu for the student. In part, too, the clinical programmes offer a kind of social welfare by supplementing the legal aid systems. There is no doubt that, especially in the large cities, the Student Legal Aid schemes fulfill a valuable social need in providing legal advice to many who would otherwise go without. Within the law schools they offer an outlet for the sense of social commitment that is shared by many students and some law teachers.

Apart from the clinical programmes there are other programmes and courses in the law schools with strong practical orientations. Almost all the law schools have a substantial number of practitioners who lecture on a part-time basis. Most law schools require students to argue a moot case (that is, a hypothetical appeal case). Moots vary greatly. Some are primarily academic exercises, but others include practical skills and in some moot programmes practitioners are heavily involved. Many law schools have courses that involve drafting exercises. To some extent the practical content of these programmes and courses is used to illuminate the academic study of the various aspects of law. To some extent, also, however, the effect of these programmes is to move university legal

---

5 *Ibid.*

education a little closer to direct professional training than formerly. The attitude of the law societies to legal education remains ambivalent, and it is uncertain to what extent Canadian law schools, under pressure from the law societies on the one side and from their own students on the other, may alter still further their present balance between the practical and theoretical side of legal education. On the other hand, there are pressures in the other direction. Closer links with other divisions of the university are leading to greater interest in the relationship of law to such subjects as economics, philosophy, history, sociology, political theory, anthropology, and linguistics. The final result of the contest between Wright and the Law Society of Upper Canada is still undecided.

CURRICULUM

The law schools, like other divisions of the university, were affected by the move towards optional curricula in the 1960s. Most law schools require students to take courses in Contracts, Torts, Property, Criminal Law, Civil Procedure and Constitutional Law (the six "core courses" listed as essential by the Law Society of Upper Canada). The bulk of these courses is usually disposed of in the first year, so that the curriculum divides into a first year of largely compulsory core courses, followed by two years of optional courses.

Many of the law schools have embellished their calendars with comparatively specialized courses, and fears were expressed by the profession that the optional curriculum would be the death of sound legal education. In fact, however, most students select the very courses that were compulsory before introduction of the optional curriculum, that is, Commercial Law, Company Law, Evidence, Family Law, Real Estate Transactions, Income Tax, Administrative Law, Wills and Trusts, and (to a lesser extent), Debtor and Creditor, and Conflicts. The selection of these courses is not surprising in view of the fact that most of them are generally agreed to be essential tools of the practising lawyer. The broad range of options in the calendar is therefore a little misleading. A student who takes all the courses listed above, together with a few advanced courses in areas of her special interest, will have little spare time for esoteric options.

Some law schools require each student to take one course of a jurisprudential nature, sometimes called a "perspective" course, that is a course designed to look at legal institutions from a broader perspective than is possible in a course in a particular area of substantive law. This has not proved to be an onerous requirement to students, but sometimes causes disagreement among the faculty on whose courses are, and whose are not, entitled to the perspective or jurisprudential designation.

Some law schools, in an attempt to introduce greater variety to the pattern of legal studies, have allowed students to write a single paper to satisfy the requirements of a group of related courses, or to carry on a private research project inside or outside the law school. The study of law always involves some research, but the aim of the developments referred to here is to enable students to engage in a fairly extensive research project, and to open the door to the possibility of empirical research. These developments have generally been welcomed, but, for the reason given above, students who wish to take all the "mainstream" courses must organize their time very carefully in order to make room for major research projects.

THE CASE METHOD

One of the characteristics of American legal education that was adopted by the Canadian law schools is the case method of instruction. The case method, as contrasted with the lecture method, requires students to read the relevant material (usually reported judgments in decided cases) before class. The instructor, instead of simply expounding her views, proceeds by a question and answer method, often called the Socratic method, to draw out from the students the significance of the case under discussion. In fact there are many variations of the case method. In its pure form the instructor never makes a statement of his view, but brings out every point that he wishes to make by means of questions. Most Canadian law teachers, however, use a mixture of the case method and the lecture method. Commonly an instructor will make a short introductory statement, ask questions about a case, then summarize the discussion and, often, put forward her own view.

Students are sometimes impatient with the case system of teaching. It does, however, have the merit of bringing home the strength of the conflicting arguments on each point. Some sort of discussion, real or simulated, is essential to the understanding of legal problems. In universities where the lecture method is used, there are almost always supplementary discussion groups in addition to the lectures. It is one thing for a student to hear that there are arguments on each side of a question and dutifully to write them down in his notes. It is another for her to *see* the case from one side, and then suddenly to see it rearrange itself like a kaleidoscope the other way around. Here is an illustration from the law of contracts. A leases a quarry from B, promising to grade the land at the end of the lease. In breach of contract he fails to grade the land. The cost of grading is $60,000, but the value of the land is $10,000 ungraded, and would be

$11,000 graded.[6] Look at the problem one way and it is perfectly obvious that B should recover $60,000. After all, she contracted for graded land, and $60,000 is what it will cost to grade the land. Further, A has no complaint, for he promised to grade the land and expected to have to incur the expense. Anyway, people should be made to keep their contracts. Look at the problem again, and it seems obvious that $1,000 is the right measure. After all, $1,000 is all B has lost. Breach of contract is not a crime. We are out to compensate B, not to give her a windfall or to punish A. A good discussion of a decided case on this problem with judicial opinion divided, can bring out the force of the conflicting arguments far more vividly than even the best lecturer.

Discussion of cases should not be confined to the classroom, and many law students find it useful to meet in groups, more or less regularly, for study and discussion.

CASE BRIEFS

Most law students find it convenient to make notes of cases they read. "Case brief" is a name sometimes given to a note of the case containing a summary of the facts, the decision and the reasons for it. Some students consider it unnecessary to make case briefs and, instead, underline key passages in their casebooks. There are, however, several reasons for making written notes. First, the act of preparing and writing a summary of a case tends to fix it more firmly in the mind. Second, brief and accurate notes are helpful for review. Third, and more importantly, making a summary of the significant facts of the case requires skill and judgment. The process of picking out the significant facts from a mass of those that are insignificant is one of the lawyer's most important skills, and the best way to learn to do it is by practice. The ability to record the significant facts and legal principles concisely and precisely is an essential tool. It is easy to say to oneself when reading a case: "Yes, I see what that is about", underline twenty per cent of the text, and pass on to the next case. The discipline of putting pen to paper, however, will often necessitate finding an answer to a number of questions that may have gone entirely unnoticed on a cursory reading. Problems, or apparent difficulties, should be noted with the case summary.

Here is part of a judgment in a case on contract damages:

LORD DENNING M.R. Mr. Jarvis is a solicitor, employed by a local authority at Barking. In 1969 he was minded to go for Christmas to Switzerland. He was looking forward to a ski-ing holiday. It is his one fortnight's holiday in the year. He prefers it in the winter rather than in the summer.

---

6 The example is based on *Groves v. John Wunder Co.*, 286 N.W. 235 (Minn. S.C., 1939).

Mr. Jarvis read a brochure issued by Swans Tours Ltd. He was much attracted by the description of Mörlialp, Giswil, Central Switzerland. I will not read the whole of it, but just pick out some of the principal attractions:

"House Party Centre with special resident host. . . . Mörlialp is a most wonderful little resort on a sunny plateau . . . Up there you will find yourself in the midst of beautiful alpine scenery, which in winter becomes a wonderland of sun, snow and ice, with a wide variety of fine ski-runs, a skating rink and exhilarating toboggan run . . . Why did we choose the Hotel Krone . . . mainly and most of all because of the 'Gemütlichkeit' and friendly welcome you will receive from Herr and Frau Weibel. . . . The Hotel Krone has its own Alphütte Bar which will be open several evenings a week. . . . No doubt you will be in for a great time, when you book this house-party holiday . . . Mr. Weibel, the charming owner, speaks English."

On the same page, in a special yellow box, it was said:

"Swans House Party in Mörlialp. All these House Party arrangements are included in the price of your holiday. Welcome party on arrival. Afternoon tea and cake for 7 days. Swiss dinner by candlelight. Fondue party. Yodler evening. Chali farewell party in the 'Alphütte Bar'. Service of representative."

Alongside on the same page there was a special note about ski-packs. "Hire of Skis, Sticks and Boots . . . Ski Tuition . . . 12 days £11.10." In August 1969, on the faith of that brochure, Mr. Jarvis booked a 15-day holiday, with ski-pack. The total charge was £63.45, including Christmas supplement. He was to fly from Gatwick to Zurich on December 20, 1969, and return on January 3, 1970.

The plaintiff went on the holiday, but he was very disappointed. He was a man of about 35 and he expected to be one of a house party of some 30 or so people. Instead, he found there were only 13 during the first week. In the second week there was no house party at all. He was the only person there. Mr. Weibel could not speak English. So there was Mr. Jarvis, in the second week, in his hotel with no house party at all, and no one could speak English, except himself. He was very disappointed, too, with the ski-ing. . . . There were only mini-skis, about 3 ft. long. So he did not get his ski-ing as he wanted to. In the second week he did get some longer skis for a couple of days, but then, because of the boots, his feet got rubbed and he could not continue even with the long skis. So his ski-ing holiday, from his point of view, was pretty well ruined.

There were many other matters, too. They appear trivial when they are set down in writing, but I have no doubt they loomed large in Mr. Jarvis's mind, when coupled with the other disappointments. He did not have the nice Swiss cakes which he was hoping for. The only cakes for tea were potato crisps and little dry nut cakes. The yodler evening consisted of one man from the locality who came in his working clothes for a little while, and sang four or five songs very quickly. The "Alphütte Bar" was an unoccupied annexe which was only open one evening. There was a representative, Mrs. Storr, there during the first week, but she was not there during the second week.

The matter was summed up by the judge:

> "During the first week he got a holiday in Switzerland which was to some extent inferior . . . and, as to the second week, he got a holiday which was very largely inferior."

to what he was led to expect.

What is the legal position? I think that the statements in the brochure were representations or warranties. The breaches of them give Mr. Jarvis a right to damages. . . .

The one question in the case is: What is the amount of damages? The judge seems to have taken the difference in value between what he paid for and what he got. He said that he intended to give "the difference between the two values and no other damages" under any other head. He thought that Mr. Jarvis had got half of what he paid for. So the judge gave him half the amount which he had paid, namely £31.72. Mr. Jarvis appeals to this court. He says that the damages ought to have been much more.
. . .

What is the right way of assessing damages? It has often been said that on a breach of contract damages cannot be given for mental distress. Thus in *Hamlin v. Great Northern Railway Co.* (1856) 1 H. & N. 408, 411 Pollock C.B. said that damages cannot be given "for the disappointment of mind occasioned by the breach of contract". And in *Hobbs v. London & South Western Railway Co.* (1875) L.R. 10 Q.B. 111, 122, Mellor J. said that

> "for the mere inconvenience, such as annoyance and loss of temper, or vexation, or for being disappointed in a particular thing which you have set your mind upon, without real physical inconvenience resulting, you cannot recover damages."

The courts in those days only allowed the plaintiff to recover damages if he suffered physical inconvenience, such as having to walk five miles home, as in *Hobbs'* case; or to live in an over-crowded house, *Bailey v. Bullock*, [1950] 2 All E.R. 1167.

I think that those limitations are out of date. In a proper case damages for mental distress can be recovered in contract, just as damages for shock can be recovered in tort. One such case is a contract for a holiday, or any other contract to provide entertainment and enjoyment. If the contracting party breaks his contract, damages can be given for the disappointment, the distress, the upset and frustration caused by the breach. I know that it is difficult to assess in terms of money, but it is no more difficult than the assessment which the courts have to make every day in personal injury cases for loss of amenities. Take the present case. Mr. Jarvis has only a fortnight's holiday in the year. He books it far ahead and looks forward to it all that time. He ought to be compensated for the loss of it.

A good illustration was given by Edmund Davies L.J. in the course of the argument. He put the case of a man who has taken a ticket for Glyndebourne. It is the only night on which he can get there. He hires a car to take him. The car does not turn up. His damages are not limited to the mere cost of the ticket. He is entitled to general damages for the disappointment he has suffered and the loss of the entertainment which he should have had. Here, Mr. Jarvis's fortnight's winter holiday has been a grave disappointment. It

is true that he was conveyed to Switzerland and back and had meals and bed in the hotel. But that is not what he went for. He went to enjoy himself with all the facilities which the defendants said he would have. He is entitled to damages for the lack of those facilities, and for his loss of enjoyment.
    . . .

I think the judge was in error in taking the sum paid for the holiday £63.45 and halving it. The right measure of damages is to compensate him for the loss of entertainment and enjoyment which he was promised, and which he did not get.
    Looking at the matter quite broadly, I think the damages in this case, should be the sum of £125. I would allow the appeal, accordingly.[7]

Some of the facts are trivial. Others are important. The important facts cannot be distilled from the opening paragraph alone; only an appreciation of the decision and its reasons can enable a reader to distinguish the significant facts. It hardly matters that Mr. Jarvis worked for the Barking municipality, or that there were potato chips for tea, but it turns out to be important that two weeks was his full annual vacation. Here is the sort of note a student might make:

J planned a ski trip abroad for his annual two-week vacation in reliance on S's travel brochure. The brochure promised physical and social attractions that did not materialize. There were no suitable skis and no house party as promised. The cost of the vacation was £63 and at trial J recovered half the cost, on the basis that he had received about half its value. On appeal to the Court of Appeal the damages were increased to £125. Lord Denning held that earlier exclusions of damages for mental distress were out of date (disappointment, distress, upset and frustration compensable) and that compensation was payable for loss of promised enjoyment. Difficulties of assessment were no bar (*cf.* personal injury cases in tort).

    [*Quaere*:

    1. Is this case compensating wounds inflicted by the breach (distress, etc.), or is it valuing the enjoyment that was promised and not given? Or both?

    2. Would this principle be restricted to defendants in the business of selling enjoyment (*i.e.*, travel agents, etc.)? What about sellers of goods, or other services?

    3. Are the assessment problems as easy as Lord Denning suggests? Is there an element of the punitive creeping in?]

It will be seen that the effort and discipline of writing this note have drawn the writer's attention to several points that might otherwise have been overlooked. Writing a note on a case compels one to ask: exactly

---

7 *Jarvis v. Swans Tours Ltd.*, [1973] Q.B. 233 at 235-238 (C.A.).

what does this case decide? Which facts were essential? How far does the principle extend? These are all important questions for an understanding of the decision. Every case should be looked at from two points of view, to discern the narrowest principle that *must* have been accepted by the court to support the decision, and to discern the widest principle that the decision *might* be subsequently held to support.[8] The use of decided cases will be discussed more fully in a later chapter.

CASEBOOKS AND TEXTBOOKS

The standard and essential tool of the case method of teaching is the "casebook", a collection of materials, generally judicial decisions, that the student is expected to read in order to prepare herself for the discussion of each case or group of cases. Sometimes a casebook is printed and published by a commercial publisher. Often, however, it is produced privately by photographic reproduction. The ease and comparatively low cost of reproduction and duplication have meant that any law teacher can have the luxury of preparing his own casebook, and many Canadian law teachers have done so.

Textbooks are what lawyers call monographs, or treatises, that is, books written generally by a single author expressing her views in a methodical manner of a particular area of the law.

Until recently, few Canadian textbooks were available, and the use of English texts was generally disapproved by Canadian law teachers. They feared that textbooks would oversimplify the law, and present it as a static set of rules to be learned. The sort of textbook they had in mind is the sort that is often disparagingly called a "black-letter law" book, a term derived from the practice still maintained in some textbooks of printing legal rules in heavy type, with explanatory comment following in lighter type. Such books were seen as incompatible with the critical analysis associated with the case method of teaching, and their use was actively discouraged.

The judges, no less than the academics, now perceive the dangers of the black-letter law books. In a recent case the House of Lords rejected a rule that had been confidently asserted through several editions by a textbook writer. Lord Wilberforce said:

> My Lords, this passage is almost a perfect illustration of the dangers, well perceived by our predecessors but tending to be neglected in modern times, of placing reliance on textbook authority for an analysis of judicial decisions. It is on the face of it a jumble of unclear propositions not logically related to each other. It is "supported" by footnote references to cases . . . which

---

8 See below, p. 78.

are not explained or analysed. It would be tedious to go through them in detail, but I am satisfied that . . . [n]either [of two cases cited in the textbook] . . . in any way bears upon one such as the present.[9]

Now, however, there are more Canadian textbooks available than formerly, and many textbooks, Canadian, English and American, make a serious attempt at critical analysis and adopt an approach very different from the black-letter books. Most law teachers have softened their opposition and many would now encourage an intelligent and critical use of textbooks. It need hardly be said that reliance on a textbook is no substitute for a student's own critical analysis of the primary legal materials.

UNIVERSITY LAW COURSES OUTSIDE THE LAW FACULTIES

In recent years a considerable interest has been shown in the study of law outside the law schools. The law schools themselves have regarded these developments with somewhat mixed feelings.

Most law schools in Canada require at least two years of university study before admission. Many law students in fact complete a degree in their undergraduate subject. The law schools do not prescribe a "pre-law" course. Law teachers are not agreed that any particular discipline constitutes an especially good preparation for the study of law. Successful students have come from every field. So far as there is a consensus it would be that rigorous thought and disciplined work in any field together with development of facility with the English language is a good preparation. Law teachers are not anxious to take students who have already studied law. The three-year LL.B. curriculum is generally thought to be long enough (some have said that it is too long.) Insofar as a rationale can be articulated for the two-year requirement of pre-law study, it is that the student should develop her skills in some other field. She will, after all, be expecting to read law for the rest of her life. The statement of the Association of American Law Schools on pre-law education, reproduced in Appendix E, would be accepted by most Canadian law teachers. It is therefore bad for the student, bad for the law faculties, and bad for the Arts faculties for future law students to undertake an extensive study of law in the Arts faculty. Experience suggests, unfortunately, that law-related courses in the Arts faculty do tend to attract potential law students.

It is sometimes said that the Arts faculties could develop programmes of legal studies where law would be studied as a "liberal art". A distinction is thus suggested between a liberal study of law appropriate to the Faculty of Arts, and the illiberal, narrow and technical study of law that presumably

---

9 *Johnson v. Agnew*, [1980] A.C. 367 at 395-6 (H.L.).

goes on at the law schools. I have suggested earlier that any serious study of law must involve a bridge between the practical and the theoretical. It is hard to envisage a satisfactory programme of legal studies that would not duplicate the law school's programme. There is, however, a case to be made for a programme of legal studies in an Arts faculty at a university that does not have its own law faculty. Such a university can make the case that it, like other universities, has a right to teach law, that location of the law programme within the Arts faculty is a mere matter of organization, and that professional recognition is not its concern.

Ironically, in some cases where Arts faculties have introduced legal courses, these have tended to be more practical and less theoretical than the corresponding courses in the law faculties. The reason is that the main courses in the law faculties are generally taught by full-time law teachers who have a commitment to a theoretical study of law and who are interested in exploring the ideas underlying the law. On the other hand, if the Arts faculty offers a course in, say, Commercial Law, it is likely to be heavily subscribed, and the only source of instructors will be practising lawyers who will teach sections of the course on a part-time basis. Practising lawyers are much more likely than academics to favour a "black-letter law" approach, and to teach the law as a set of rules, the learning of which is relieved by a few anecdotes. So the "liberal arts" approach is quite likely in practice to be considerably less liberal than the law schools themselves, and to be positively harmful to the prospective law student.

These considerations tend to suggest caution in introducing extensive programmes of legal studies in Arts faculties. It must be conceded, however, that there are good reasons for teaching and studying some law in the Arts faculty and that there are legally orientated courses of the highest standards in the Arts faculties. One reason is the need to include a legal dimension in a group of related courses on some aspect of society. For example, a programme of courses in Criminology, Industrial Relations, Environmental Protection or Canadian Native People, will each need some kind of legal component. Political Science, Constitutional History, Philosophy, Sociology, and Commerce can hardly be seriously tackled without an element of law. It can also be argued that there is a place for a general course to offer some sort of introduction to the legal system, to ideas of law and to legal reasoning. This would be primarily designed for those not planning to go on to law school, but it would be hard to justify the exclusion of a student who wanted an introduction to legal ideas in order to test his own interest in and aptitude for further legal study. With the study of law increasing at the high school level, it is likely that there will be increasing interest in the subject also in the universities.

LAW SCHOOL ADMISSIONS

One of the most important administrative tasks of a law faculty is to select students from the applicants for admission. A law school admissions committee attempts primarily to choose the best possible group of students for the school. As a decision-making body in a public institution, however, the committee owes a duty to each applicant to treat him fairly in comparison with every other applicant.

Many readers will be familiar with a test called the Law School Admission Test (LSAT) administered by an American organization called the Educational Testing Service. Most common law schools in Canada require applicants to take the test. Undoubtedly this requirement places a burden on applicants. The attraction of the test to admission committees is that it provides a common basis for a reasonably fair comparison of applicants from different universities and different degree courses. It is difficult to envisage a satisfactory alternative. Interviews, for example, even if feasible, would not necessarily be fair to all applicants. For this reason alone, the LSAT is likely to remain popular with admission committees.

The law schools differ in the weight they attach to the LSAT. No school relies on it exclusively. Some use undergraduate grades as the primary test, and the LSAT only secondarily, to distinguish borderline cases. Others claim to look at all the information together. Others reduce the undergraduate record and the LSAT score by a weighted formula to a single figure. In any of these cases the importance of the test score is considerable. Grade inflation in the undergraduate faculties means that hundreds of applicants have quite similar records. It is almost impossible to compare different courses at different universities. Letters of reference are predictable and uninformative in most cases. The LSAT is the only ready means of making a reasonably fair distinction among such applicants. Even law schools that claim to use the test only in "borderline" cases may give it as much weight as other schools if most applicants are treated as "borderline". Where so-called mature students are considered without undergraduate university study, the LSAT tends to assume an even greater importance.

It has been occasionally suggested that the law schools should operate some kind of personality test to distinguish the best potential lawyers. The drawback to such a proposal is that there is no agreed set of characteristics that make up the ideal lawyer, and no reliable test for detecting them. We must remember that the law schools are dealing with some of the most capable students in Canada. I have greater faith in the ability of potential law students to see through any supposed character test than in the ability of the law schools to design such a test.

Applicants are frequently concerned about preparation for the LSAT. The Educational Testing Service publishes a brochure in which it advises that specific knowledge is not required:

> The LSAT is designed to measure certain mental abilities important in the study of law and, thus, to aid law schools in assessing the academic promise of their applicants. The test covers a broad range of academic disciplines and is intended to give no advantage to candidates from a particular academic background. The questions yielding the LSAT score are designed to measure the ability to read, understand, and reason.[10]

A sample set of test questions is given in the brochure, with full explanation and discussion. Considerable emphasis is placed on grammar, spelling, and English usage, presumably on the basis that all of the lawyer's skills involve the use of words, and that those who are good with words tend to be good also at law. The sample test exhibits no sign of American bias, except insofar as names of American cities and states are used in some of the questions. There is now no test of "general knowledge".

A number of courses are offered by private enterprises that claim to prepare candidates for the LSAT. The law schools disapprove of these courses, but cannot effectively stop them. There is some evidence that a candidate's score tends to increase if she takes the test twice, the reason presumably being that she comes to the second test familiar with the type of question to be asked. Possibly the preparation courses, if they do nothing else, give the candidate some experience of the type of questions to be asked. They might, therefore, be expected to have the same effect as a practice test. The law schools have been cautious in making public statements about preparation courses. Though irritated that private enterprises should be trading for profit on the concern of applicants and making the law schools, as it were, unwilling partners, the schools must be careful not to make statements that might be untrue. It would be unwise, for instance, to announce that the courses do no good; they may well do as much good as a practice test. Again, if the law schools threatened to discount any score obtained after a preparation course, they would be setting a trap for the incautious, and an invitation to lie for the dishonest. The law schools disapprove of the courses in either event. If effective, they distort the admissions process and cast doubt on the reliability of the LSAT itself; if ineffective, they are misleading and exploiting applicants for private profit. But there is very little that the schools can do to remedy the situation, short of abandoning the test altogether.

The LSAT brochure makes this cautious comment on preparation courses:

---

10   1982 Law School Admission Services, p. 3.

LSAC and LSAS strive to offer a test which is as free from potential effects of short term preparation courses as possible. Efforts are made in the design and construction of the LSAT to minimize possible effects preparation courses may have on an examinee's test scores. To date LSAC/LSAS have not been able to construct a definitive study which would establish that such courses either improve or do not improve an examinee's scores on average.[11]

In recent years many law schools have announced a relaxation of ordinary requirements for "mature" applicants, and in some cases for applicants from economically deprived backgrounds or from disadvantaged racial minority groups. The philosophies underlying support for admission of these special groups vary, as would be expected, with the social and political philosophies of those giving their support. Some see admission to law school as a means of effecting to some extent a transfer of power or wealth from one group in society to another, or a means of righting some of the wrongs of the past. A widely-held view is, however, that special admissions can be justified on a more modest basis, namely, that the individuals admitted are to be of equal merit with others but that the assessment of their merit may take into account any relevant adverse circumstances that they may have had to overcome, or that may have affected the standard measurements of their merit. Roger Carter, Q.C., then the Director of the Native Law Centre at the University of Saskatchewan said of the native students who graduate from the Saskatchewan preparatory programme:

> In considering these students for admission, Canadian law schools resort to discretionary policies forming part of their regular admission procedures. These policies are of long standing and have nothing to do with race or ancestry. In deciding whether or not to exercise this discretionary power a law school will consider a number of factors which, in the ordinary way, are not taken into account. These will include the individual's work and social experience, evidence of motivation and drive, community leadership, commitment to education and other matters which may indicate that the applicant has sufficient maturity and potential to deal successfully with law studies even though he or she may not be able to meet ordinary *academic* requirements. It is under this kind of admission policy that mature applicants are considered for entry. In the case of native students who have taken the Saskatchewan program an additional, and significant, factor which the law school will take into account is successful completion of the course. Where ultimately an affirmative decision is made by the law school to admit such a student to first-year law, under its discretionary policy, then that student is regarded as being equally qualified with other students.[12]

This view, like most workable compromises, has the virtue of maintaining intact a principle seen to be important and equitable (admis-

---

11 *Ibid.*
12 The National, August 1978, p. 10.

sion on the basis of individual merit) while allowing in practice some departure in specific cases. The debate on the issue of admission policies for racial minorities, which came before the Supreme Court of the United States in 1978,[13] shows, incidentally, the elusive quality of general concepts of justice in reaching difficult decisions. To some, justice plainly requires preference for members of deprived minority groups; to others it plainly requires equal treatment of applicants. Justice, equality, abhorrence of racial discrimination, are general principles to which everyone subscribes. But general principles do not decide concrete cases.

In many law schools the regional origin of the applicant is taken into account, and open preference is given to local candidates. Such discrimination seems regrettable, and contrary to the principle of admission on merit. In view of the provincial funding of university education, and the enormous competition for places in law school, regional discrimination is perhaps inevitable.

All Canadian common law schools normally require a minimum of two years' university work before law school. Some law schools give express preference to applicants with degrees. In Ontario, however, a significant number of applicants are admitted without degrees, the general attitude of admissions committees being assessment on individual merit. Even on this basis it is likely that most law students will continue to have pre-law degrees, for most students, having put in two years towards a B.A., will wish to complete the degree.

REASONS FOR STUDYING LAW

Everyone will tell the aspiring law student that the profession is now overcrowded. One thousand lawyers are called to the bar each year in Ontario, where in 1965 the total number of practitioners was only 6000.[14] Articling positions and offers of employment are not always easy to obtain, particularly in the large cities. Lawyers who had hoped to practise with a large firm in Toronto are being driven to open up on their own in smaller towns. A law degree is no guarantee of wealth or even of secure employment.

None of this, however, can be decisive to the person who has made up his mind that he wants to study law. Nor should it be. There is always room for good lawyers, and the universities will always welcome good students. It is to be remembered that there are many varieties of legal practice, and many other careers in which a legal training will prove useful.

---

13 *Bakke v. Regents of the University of California*, 98 S. Ct. 2733 (1978).
14 In 1992 the number was about 24,500.

Every year law schools admit a few students who ought not to have applied. These are often students who have succeeded very well in another field, and have drifted into law for one of a variety of reasons: they could not think of an alternative career; they were convinced that there were too many Ph.D.s in their former discipline; friends were going to law school; relatives pressed them to go; the admission to law school was a prize worth having for its own sake as a badge of intellectual superiority. I would urge any readers of this book who might be pressed by such reasons to resist them. If you find the examples of legal reasoning given in this book dull, or if they seem unrelated to anything of real value and importance, or if you think that detailed discussion and the drawing of subtle distinctions between cases is a waste of time, you may well be a wiser person than the writer of this book. But the study of law is not likely to suit you.

ADMISSION TO PRACTICE

Admission to the practice of law is entirely in the hands of the governing bodies of the profession in each province (Law Society or Barristers' Society). The regulations vary from province to province, but the general requirement is a law degree from a Canadian common law school, followed by twelve months of articling under the supervision of a lawyer practising in the province. Ontario has a further requirement of a course of lectures and examinations (the teaching portion of the Bar Admission Course). A common law degree is, therefore, "portable", in the sense that a graduate of any Canadian common law school is in general eligible to article and to be admitted to practice in any province. Some provinces have particular requirements, however, and a student considering the possibility of studying law in one province and articling in another should ensure that her proposed course of study will be satisfactory to the professional governing body of the province where she proposes to article.[15]

---

15 There are restrictions on interprovincial transfer of qualified lawyers. See below, p. 122.

3

THE LANGUAGE OF THE LAW

LEGAL LANGUAGE

Some suppose that the lawyer's job is to learn as many long words as possible, preferably in Latin and Law French, so as to make himself incomprehensible. Presumably, the harder he is to understand the better he must be as a lawyer. Nothing could be further from the truth. The good lawyer expresses herself with clarity, simplicity and brevity.

Every task that a lawyer performs requires the use of language. Whether he is arguing in court or drawing documents or giving written or oral advice, the lawyer must have the ability to translate his meaning effectively into words. The best preparation for the study of law is to acquire the ability to write the English language quickly and effectively. The student who commences the study of law with the ability to express her ideas quickly and clearly in writing starts with a very great advantage.

George Bernard Shaw wrote that all professions are conspiracies against the laity,[1] and no doubt the legal profession has earned its reputation for obscurantism. Generations of legal drafters have refused to let their clients simply give something to someone if they can give, devise and bequeath all their right title and interest in it. But, sanctified formulas apart, the best legal writing is the simplest.

The same is true of judicial opinions. Some judges write obscurely, but the best speak and write clearly and simply. Lord Denning, one of the best known judges of modern times, is notorious for the clipped simplicity of his style. One of his judgments begins: "It happened on April 19, 1964. It was bluebell time in Kent."[2] Another: "Broadchalke is one of the most pleasing villages in England. Old Herbert Bundy, the defendant,

---

1 G.B. Shaw, *The Doctor's Dilemma* (1906), Act. 1.
2 *Hinz v. Berry*, [1970] 2 Q.B. 40 at 42 (C.A.).

was a farmer there."[3] Compare this with the more usual sort of introductory statement: "This is an application by the surviving executor of the estate of the late Sam Finkle for the opinion, advice and direction of the Court, and for answers to certain questions posed on the notice of motion."[4] Lord Denning's style of opening sentence is perhaps a trifle less factually informative, but it comes as a welcome change to the jaded reader of law reports.

THE LANGUAGE OF LITIGATION

The parties to an ordinary civil action are called the plaintiff and defendant in the court where proceedings commence (the court of first instance) and the appellant and respondent on appeal. If the party initiating the proceedings is applying for a particular order he is generally called the applicant, and the other party the respondent. In divorce cases it is petitioner and respondent. A case is known by the names of the parties. So, if Smith sues Jones then the case is known as *Smith v. Jones.* The *v.* stands for the Latin word, "versus", meaning against. It is usual in Canada, as in England, to pronounce the name of the case as "Smith and Jones", but it is also correct to say, "Smith against Jones".

Criminal cases are called, for example, *Regina v. Smith*, or *R. v. Smith*, which can be pronounced just as written or, more formally, called "The Queen against Smith" or, of course, at the appropriate dates, "The King against Smith". If the accused appeals to the Supreme Court of Canada the case will become *Smith v. The Queen.* In referring to the Queen as a party to criminal proceedings, however, one always speaks of "The Crown". It is very common and convenient practice in writing and speaking of criminal law cases to use only the name of the accused. Then the question of which party appealed can be forgotten and English cases, which may be *D.P.P.* (Director of Public Prosecutions) *v. Smith* and American cases which may be *People* or *Commonwealth v. Smith*, can all be cited simply as *Smith.* It is acceptable style to write "the rule in *Smith*" or "the rule in *Smith's* case". The words "et al." are usually omitted in giving the name of a case, but, if included, should be spoken in English ("and another" or "and others").

CITING CASES IN LEGAL WRITING

Where a case is reported in several series of reports, it is not necessary to cite every series. An Alberta case on the law of torts, for example,

---

3 *Lloyds Bank Ltd. v. Bundy*, [1975] Q.B. 326 at 334 (C.A.).
4 *Re Finkle* (1977), 82 D.L.R. (3d) 445 at 446 (Man. Q.B.).

might well be reported in the Alberta Reports, Western Weekly Reports, Supreme Court Reports, Dominion Law Reports, National Reports and Canadian Cases on the Law of Torts. Where the case is reported in the Supreme Court Reports, this citation should always be given, the Supreme Court Reports being an official series published by the government. Similarly, Ontario cases are generally cited from the Ontario Reports, this being regarded as a semi-official series privately published, but by the authority of the Law Society. After that, the general rule is one of convenience, citation being given to the series to which the reader is most likely to have convenient access. Most Canadian law libraries do not possess the American state reports. Citation to the unofficial National Reporter Series is therefore generally acceptable in Canadian Legal writing, though an American journal would insist on citation of the state reports first. In citing English cases the semi-official Law Reports citation is always to be preferred. Other series need not be added unless, as, for example, in note 12 on page 105 below, there is some significant difference in the reports.

Where there are two or more plaintiffs or defendants, the name of the first only is usually given in legal writing. So *The Great Canadian Railway Company Ltd. and Joseph Higgins v. Jacob Smith and Emily Stick, Zachariah Zubb third party*, should be cited as *Great Canadian Railway Co. Ltd. v. Smith.* The name of the corporation should be given in full (abbreviations "Co." and "Ltd." are acceptable) the first time the case is mentioned in a piece of legal writing; thereafter the case can be referred to in any convenient way, *e.g.* the *Canadian Railway* case or the *Smith* case or *Canadian Railway v. Smith* or *G.C.R. v. Smith.* In cases involving ships, it is common to call the case by the name of the ship involved, which is usually a little snappier than the name of the Swiss corporation that may own it. Individuals are usually referred to by their last names only, except where, as in Criminal law cases, to avoid confusion, *Smith (Roger)* must be distinguished from *Smith (John).* Sometimes it is necessary to add the date; *Smith (John, 1959).* Law reports often include the words "et al." ("and another", or "and others") in the style of cause where there are multiple parties. The words "et al." are not usually included in case citations in legal writing. The word "versus" (against) never appears in full. Names of cases are underlined or italicized in Canadian legal writing.

CIVIL LITIGATION

Pleadings is the name given to formal statements of the parties that precede the court hearing in civil litigation. Their object is to define as many as possible of the issues before trial. Proceedings usually start with a Statement of Claim (or, in older cases, a declaration, bill, complaint, petition or prayer), to which the defendant makes a Statement of Defence. If she has her own complaint against the other party she can enter a counterclaim. Before trial there is an opportunity, called Discovery, of questioning the other party to the action and for compelling the production of relevant documents. These pre-trial procedures, though designed to save time and expense at trial, often give rise to disputes in themselves (called "interlocutory" proceedings) and a disputed point arising out of the proceedings might even go to the Supreme Court of Canada. Often the key question of law in a case arises at the interlocutory stage. In a famous Scottish case the pursuer (Scottish name for plaintiff, the other party being the defender) alleged that she had been made ill by consuming a contaminated bottle of ginger beer manufactured by the defender (she alleged that there was a snail in the bottle). The defender objected that even if these facts were proved he could not be liable, that is, that the Statement of Claim disclosed no cause of action. The case went to the House of Lords (the highest court for England and Scotland) on this issue and is famous for establishing that a manufacturer is liable to a person injured by a negligently manufactured product and, more widely, that persons are generally responsible for negligent injuries they cause to others. But it never was judicially established that there actually was a snail in the bottle.[5]

In former times it was essential for pleadings to be exactly correct and for the plaintiff to bring his case exactly within a recognized kind of claim (the form of action). Modern judges reserve a liberal power of permitting amendments to pleadings, even retrospectively, provided it can be done with fairness to both parties. The plaintiff ought no longer to lose her case because she misstates the legal nature of her claim. She is entitled to an adjudication on the merits, and if her claim is meritorious she should win. As an English judge said in a slightly different context: "When these ghosts of the past stand in the path of justice clanking their mediaeval chains the proper course for the judge is to pass through them undeterred."[6]

The reasons given by judges for their conclusions are generally called "judgments" in England and Canada, but they are also sometimes known as "reasons" or "opinions", the more common American usages. "Judgment" is also the name given to the formal order of the court, for example, that A pay B $1,000.

---

5 *M'Alister (or Donoghue) v. Stevenson*, [1932] A.C. 562 (H.L.). In Scottish cases the maiden name of a married woman appears first, with her married name in brackets. The case can be cited by its full name, or as *Donoghue v. Stevenson* (the usual style). *M'Alister v. Stevenson* is not used.

6 Lord Atkin in *United Australia Ltd. v. Barclay's Bank Ltd.*, [1941] A.C. 1 at 29 (H.L.).

FRENCH AND LATIN PHRASES

In mediaeval England when French was the language of the upper classes it was also the language of the law courts, and a form of French, often called Law French, continued to be used in law reports as late as the seventeenth century. It is interesting, in light of the recent language debate in Canada, to reflect that it is only a few hundred years since the English threw off the dominance of the French language in legal matters. Law French in its latter days was an odd mixture of French, Latin and English, and reports written in the language make strange reading today. A well-known example is a case reported in 1631:

> Richardsons ch. Just. de C. Banc al Assises at Salisbury in Summer 1631, fuit assault per prisoner la condemne pur felony que puis son condemnation ject un Brickbat a le dit Justice que narrowly mist, & pur ceo immediately fuit Indictment drawn per Noy envers le prisoner, & son dexter manus ampute & fix al Gibbet sur que luy mesme immediatement hange in presence de Court.[7]

A few French phrases survive in modern legal usage. The pronunciation often differs from modern French, but this is not always because of the ignorance of lawyers. In many cases the legal pronunciation preserves the Norman French pronunciation that has dropped out of use in modern French. An example is the word "oyez" (hear!), which is still in England pronounced "Oh yes", though in Canada the influence of modern French seems to have suppressed the final consonant. Final consonants are also preserved in the phrases *autrefois acquit* and *autrefois convict* (defences to criminal charges of previous acquittal or conviction). French expressions in common legal use are listed in Appendix B.

A number of Latin phrases have come into legal use, mostly in the nineteenth century, as a consequence of the interest of the time in Roman law and the widespread knowledge of Latin among judges and lawyers. A list of those in common use is contained in Appendix A. Latin words are pronounced by lawyers as though they were English, not in the way now current among classical scholars. Lawyers, in adhering to this pronunciation, preserve the older English usage ("Caesar" and "Cicero") that was established long before classical scholars attempted to convert us to "Kaisar" and "Kikero". In one of A.P. Herbert's mock cases included in the amusing collection, *Uncommon Law,* counsel applied for relief on the ground that an order of an inferior tribunal was "ooltrah weerayze".

The Court:	Are you a Welshman, Mr. Wick?
Mr. Wick:	No, my Lord.
The Court:	Then why do you not make yourself more plain? What do you

---

7 *Anon.* (1631), 2 Dyer 188b, n.

	mean by "ooltrah weerayze" . . . Are they patent medicines or foreign potentates? So far the Court has no idea to what your application is directed.
Mr. Wick:	My Lord, *ooltrah weerayze* — "beyond the powers" — .
The Court:	Can it be that you have in mind the Latin expression *ultra vires*?
Mr. Wick:	No, My Lord; I never heard that expression before.[8]

The court then proceeds to tell Mr. Wick what it thinks of the new pronunciation of Latin, as it was then called. Fortunately, since most law students now know no Latin at all, the problem of mispronunciation has diminished considerably.

The use of Latin phrases is in any case in decline, and for good reason. The Latin language can on occasion obscure clear thought by giving a learned and authoritative appearance to a thought that, if expressed in the vernacular, would seem unbearably trite and perhaps even wrong. Latin phrases are acceptable when they have a clear meaning. When they do not, the safer course is to express one's thoughts in English. If they do not sound sufficiently impressive in that language, perhaps there is something wrong with the thoughts. A Scottish judge said of a Latin phrase (*"Res ipsa loquitur"*) "If that phrase had not been in Latin, nobody would have called it a principle. The day for canonizing Latin phrases has gone past."[9] That was in 1923.

---

8 A.P. Herbert, *Uncommon Law*, 1935, pp. 360-1, *Rex v. Venables and Others: The Dead Pronunciation.*

9 Lord Shaw of Dunfermline in *Ballard v. North British Ry. Co.*, [1923] S.C. 43 at 56 (H.L. Scot.).

4

ANALYZING LEGAL PROBLEMS

CLARITY

The most important advice to any lawyer in giving an opinion or to any law student in analyzing a legal problem at law school, is to write clearly. Avoid complex syntax. Do not hesitate to use two sentences if subordinate clauses threaten to become unmanageable. In legal writing clarity should never be sacrificed to elegance; clarity in legal writing is the arbiter of elegance. Be as brief as possible, but not at the expense of clarity. Add an extra sentence if it makes your analysis easier to follow. Avoid legal jargon such as Latin tags that obscure rather than illuminate. Avoid also sociological, economic and every other sort of jargon. Do not describe a legal dispute as a conflict situation, and do not talk about parameters unless you *really* need those terms to clarify your argument, in which case you will have to explain and define them. When expressing your own view, make it clear what that view is. Consider this conclusion:

> In my opinion there is no real answer to the arguments in favour of A. However, B has a good chance of winning in court.

The reader is left without any illumination as to what the writer's view is. Moreover, she has tried to suggest, without actually saying so, that her view might differ from the court's. But she does not explain why or how. The writer of this passage has not made up her mind about the question, but she adopts a pretentious form of words that seems to suggest that the question has been carefully considered. If you cannot make up your mind on a question, stop writing (or better still don't yet have started), and ask why it seems difficult. Then say that it is difficult. Develop the arguments on each side, say what you think the court would (in your opinion) decide, and then add your own comments, with reasons, on the merits or otherwise of that conclusion. The reader will then know: (a) that you see why it is a difficult question; (b) what you think the law is; and (c) what you think the law should be, and why. Even if the reader disagrees with your opinion on (b) and (c), the analysis will be far superior to a fudging of the issue by choice of a verbal formula that obscures your meaning.

CRITICAL ANALYSIS

The task of the student of law is not just to learn rules, but to understand them, and understanding requires critical analysis. I suggested earlier that the maxim that like cases must be decided alike is fundamental to the structure of legal reasoning. The maxim is not self-applying. No two cases are alike in all respects. When we say that like cases should be decided alike, we mean that cases lacking rationally relevant differences should be decided alike. But it is rarely obvious what differences are relevant. There will often be disagreement about whether case A is analogous to case B or whether there are essential differences.

Consider the problem mentioned earlier of the sale by a non-owner. In the case where B steals A's watch and sells it to C, A can recover her watch even if C buys for value and in good faith. What if B is not an ordinary thief but a "confidence trickster" who manages to persuade A that he (B) is a respectable citizen with ample assets and that his cheque is as good as his cash? As in the first example, he sells the watch to C who buys for value in good faith. B is never seen again but his cheque is, with the addition of the informative letters "NSF". Here, the result is different. A will not recover the watch from C. The reason given by the courts is, in essence, that there was a contract between A and B whereby the watch became B's. Consequently, unlike the case of theft by a stranger, the watch was B's to sell to C, and, in turn, became C's.

Now take a third case. Suppose that B tells a slightly different story to A. He falsely says that he is the Reverend James Chasuble, a well-known and eminently respectable clergyman. A, who does not know Mr. Chasuble, but has heard of him, takes the cheque and parts with his watch, as in the last example. Is this a case to be decided like the first or the second? Some judges have decided this case in favour of A, on the ground that since A meant to contract with Mr. Chasuble and not with the rogue B, there is no contract with B, so the watch never becomes his nor, in turn, can it become C's.

It is the task of the law student first to understand the reasoning of the decided cases on an issue of this sort, and, secondly, to subject it to critical analysis. Perhaps the reasons given by the courts are not entirely persuasive. Perhaps even the framework of the court's analysis points us in the wrong direction. Can it really be right that C's rights should depend on which particular brand of confidence trick B chose to practise on A? Perhaps the judges have been looking at the wrong criterion in making everything depend on the validity of a contract between A and B. Is there another approach that offers a more satisfactory criterion? The judges say cases 1 and 3 are alike because in neither is there a contract between A and B. But might it not be usefully said that cases 2 and 3 are alike, in that in both cases A has voluntarily entrusted his watch to B for the purpose of selling it? Might not this offer a more rational approach than the concentration on contract? Perhaps a new rule of law could be evolved, ignoring contract, but providing that one who voluntarily entrusts goods to another (at least for the purpose of sale) should take the risk of the other's dishonestly selling the goods to an innocent third party. This solution might be supported by the consideration that it is A who seeks to profit by parting with possession and that it is A who is generally in the better position to avoid the loss by choosing a worthy recipient of her trust.

This discussion, of course, is not intended to instruct the reader in the law relating to transfer of title of goods. It is intended merely to illustrate the critical approach of a good law student. This kind of critical approach is not just an academic exercise. It will strengthen the student's understanding of the existing law and will equip him to argue persuasively for a change when the occasion arises. It is by just such restatements of the principle underlying a line of cases that the common law develops. One day a lawyer will make such an argument, and the Supreme Court of Canada will accept it.

RESERVING CONCLUSIONS

In analyzing a legal problem do not jump to a conclusion in your first sentence. The danger is that this approach will lead you to adopt a defensive posture and undervalue the arguments that lead in the other direction. Consider this example from the law of contracts:

> A agrees to repair B's old car for $50.00 but fails to do so. B has to pay $200.00 to get the repairs done elsewhere, but the repairs increase the value of the car by only $20.00 from $80.00 (damaged) to $100.00 (repaired). Advise A.

Here is a sample analysis:

> B is only entitled to $20.00 because that is all she has really lost. Although she has spent $200.00 to repair the car the facts show that this was an unreasonable expenditure as she ought to have sold the car and bought a similar one in good condition for $20.00 more.

The trouble with this answer is that it undervalues the weight of the argument that B can make. B's main argument is reduced to a concessive subordinate clause. A better approach is to develop the argument for each side, and only then to express your opinion. Imagine yourself arguing for B, and put the argument as forcibly as you can, even though you may think it is wrong. You will often find that the process of developing the argument for what you consider the weaker side leads you to see that there is rather more in it than you first thought.

ARGUING FROM FIRST PRINCIPLES

Another useful precept is to develop your arguments from first principles. Do not hesitate to use simple language and to build up the argument step by step. It is almost never a mistake to be too simple. On the other hand, if you omit seemingly simple steps in the argument, you may miss an important point. Take the example just given of the car repair contract, and consider this approach:

> The object in assessing damages for breach of contract is to put the party complaining in as good a position, so far as money can do it, as if the contract had been fulfilled. What is that position on these facts? B will argue that he was promised repair of his car. Had the contract been fulfilled he would have had his car repaired, and it will cost him $200.00 to put himself in that position. Presumably, he saves the contract price of $50.00, which I assume is not paid in advance. Consequently, his damages should be measured at $150.00. A, on the other hand, will argue for a lesser measure, while fully accepting the initial proposition that damages should put B in as good a position as though the contract had been fulfilled. His argument will be that, had the contract been fulfilled, B would have had a car worth $100.00. Because of the breach B has a car worth only $80.00. Consequently, his loss is only $20.00. Again, I assume that B saves the contract price of $50.00 so, if A's argument is accepted, B will have suffered no loss at all and will be entitled only to nominal damages.

This is not a complete answer to the problem, but it is a good introduction. The basic legal principle is stated and the basic arguments for each side are built up step by step. It is a mistake to think that these points are too elementary to be worth making. They are essential to a development of the arguments. The effect of approaching the problem in this way is to cause the reader, and probably the writer as well, to appreciate the force of the argument for B. Note that the argument is carried through to its conclusion, even to the simple arithmetic required. This clarifies the scope of the two positions and, as the reader will have noticed, saves the writer from an oversight committed by the hypothetical writer of the first sample answer given above. That writer, it will be recalled, hastily jumped to the conclusion that $20.00 was the correct measure, but, as the second analysis shows, the logic of A's argument leads to nominal damages (a token amount where no loss is proved) only. Elementary step-by-step analysis is often a benefit to the writer as well as to the reader.

FORMAT OF ANALYSIS

Incidentally, in answering hypothetical problems, do not allow your answer to vary in substance according to the formal request made by the problem-setter. In the car repair case you were asked to advise A, but the substance of your answer should be exactly the same whether you are asked to advise A or to advise B or to advise the parties or to write an opinion or a memorandum or to discuss the problem or to write a judgment or to advise on an appeal. Any good analysis for any of these purposes must recognize the strength of both sides of the argument. If asked to "advise A", do not write as though to a lay client, who knows no law. The model should be a counsel's opinion, addressed to A's solicitor.

USE OF DECIDED CASES

Use of decided cases requires care and discrimination. Some law teachers advise students, in answering problems, that citation of cases is unnecessary or even undesirable. Some teachers say they are only interested in principles. Certainly indiscriminate citation of cases can be useless or worse than useless, but no law teacher can object to citation of relevant cases with due attention to distinctions between the cases cited and the problem at hand. In my view the skilful use of decided cases can illuminate analysis and is an important part of the lawyer's ability.

Consider again the car repair problem. There is an Oklahoma case holding that, on breach of a contract to restore a strip mining site, the plaintiff was entitled only to the increase in the value of the restored land and not to the much higher cost of actually effecting restoration.[1] The citation of this case will improve the answer, but it is useless simply to name the case as though it settled the issue for A, and worse than useless if knowledge of the case leads the writer to suppress the development of B's argument. By all means cite the Oklahoma case in support of A's argument, but then stop to consider any possibly relevant distinctions.

A moment's thought reveals two distinctions. First, B evidently has a personal interest in this particular car that leads her to make an "uneconomic" expenditure on it, whereas it can be assumed that the Oklahoma plaintiff's interest in the strip mining site was purely commercial. A person might have a legitimate interest in repairing an old car for personal use even though the used car market might not recognize

---

1 *Peevyhouse v. Garland Coal & Mining Co.*, 382 P. 2d 109 (Okla. S.C., 1963).

it in financial terms. Of course, A's point is still arguable. The law perhaps cannot or should not recognize such non-economic interests. It may be unreasonable; it may be foolishly sentimental. But the distinction should be recognized and the arguments developed.

Second, in the car repair case, B has actually spent the $200.00 on effecting the repairs. In the Oklahoma strip mining case the plaintiff had not restored the land and plainly would not be expected to spend the proceeds of the judgment for that purpose. In other words, the Oklahoma plaintiff was seeking what might be called a windfall at the defendant's expense. The same cannot be said of B in the car repair case, who has already spent the money. Again, this distinction may not be significant. But on the other hand it may be and the point should be developed. Now, if the reference to the Oklahoma case leads the writer to develop these points, the reference is positively helpful and improves the analysis greatly. If thinking of the Oklahoma case should lead the writer to jump to the conclusion that A's case is unanswerable and that B's arguments are not worth further thought, it would have been better forgotten.

Here is another brief example from criminal law. The facts of *R. v. Dudley and Stephens* [2] have been mentioned earlier.[3] It will be recalled that two men adrift in an open boat killed and ate a boy in order to avoid starvation. The case, once read, cannot be forgotten, and it is rightly considered the leading case on the defence of necessity. Hypothetical problems on the defence of necessity take many forms. Here are some old chestnuts:

> 1. A and V, survivors of a shipwreck, are clinging to a plank that will only support the weight of one. A pushes V off and he drowns.

> 2. A and V are mountaineers roped together. V slips and falls, A cuts the rope to save himself, and V falls to his death.

> 3. A, the captain of a ship that is in danger of sinking, orders the watertight doors to be locked closed, and V, whom A knew to be behind the doors, is drowned.

Dudley and Stephens is well worth citing in any of these questions, but there are differences between that case and each of the three hypothetical problems. In numbers 1 and 2, V is, by his own weight, actually threatening A's life, in the first case voluntarily and in the second involuntarily. In number 3 there are presumably other lives, perhaps many other lives, to save beside A's. Further, A, as captain, owes a special duty to the ship's company. Further, in 2 and 3, there is no choice as to who

---

2   (1884), 14 Q.B.D. 273.
3   Above p. 4.

should die. It is V alone or V and others. In *Dudley and Stephens*, as in problem 1, there is a choice. V, like the cabin boy, could have been saved by the sacrifice of A's life. These points may or may not be decisive — perhaps in the end you will reject the distinctions as insignificant. But the points should be noted and their significance discussed. If reference to *Dudley and Stephens* assists the development of these points it is well worth citing. But if it leads you to jump to the glib conclusion that A has no defence in any of the cases, it would have been better left uncited.

FACTS IN HYPOTHETICAL PROBLEMS

A hypothetical problem may contain facts that you consider surprising. If an event is stated as a fact, do not speculate on its probability or ask how it could have been proved. Accept it as given. If you find this difficult, reflect that the facts of many decided cases are stranger than any fiction. Moreover, in criminal appeals, for example, the correctness of a direction to the jury must be judged on the basis of assumed facts that are sometimes improbable. Suppose a judge directs the jury that the accused is to be convicted of possession of heroin if heroin is found in her pocket, whether or not she knew that it was there. On appeal from a conviction, the accused argues that this is a misdirection, because if she did not know that the heroin was in her pocket, she ought not to be convicted of possession of it. Things do not usually get in people's pockets without their knowledge. But the appellate court will judge the correctness of the direction on the assumption, however unlikely, that the heroin might have got into the accused's pocket without her knowledge.[4] The accused is entitled to have the jury determine whether or not she knew the heroin was there, and if the jury is misdirected, that right is taken away.

Consequently, if you are asked to analyze a problem where it is stated as a fact that heroin was in the accused's pocket without his knowledge, accept that as a fact. Do not say that in your view heroin cannot get into people's pockets without their knowledge, or that you do not believe the accused's story, or that the accused would never persuade a jury. If it is stated as a fact, accept it as proved. Similarly, when analyzing an appellate case on such a problem, do not be distracted by your personal opinion that the accused in the case was, in point of fact, guilty. Concentrate on the question whether the right direction was given on the assumption that the heroin might have got into his pocket without his knowledge. Again, if the facts say that a ship discharged bunker oil into a harbour, and it was set alight by a spark from a welder's torch, do not display your scientific knowledge by talking about flash points and specific gravity so as to prove

---

4 This example is based on *Beaver v. The Queen* (1957), 118 C.C.C. 129 (S.C.C.).

that it is impossible for floating bunker oil to catch fire. If you are told that it did catch fire, accept as a fact that it did. (This example is based on an actual case in which the expert evidence was that floating oil could not be expected to burn. But it did.[5] Of course, the fact that the consequence was unforeseeable is relevant to the question of liability.)

Often facts will be omitted from a problem. In that case, do not speculate as to what they may be. Consider all reasonable possibilities. Consider the first necessity problem given earlier of the persons clinging to the floating plank. We are not told whether A or V reached the plank first. It may not be relevant, but on the other hand, it may be. So an analysis should consider the situation: (1) on the assumption that A reached the plank first; and (2) on the assumption that V reached the plank first. Only reasonable possibilities need be considered in this way. For example it is not necessary to consider the case on the assumption that A is V's father, or that they are brother and sister, or that they earlier had a quarrel, or that one stands to inherit under the other's will, or on the assumption that the incident takes place outside Canadian territorial waters. There is only a common sense guide here. Some variations are fairly within the scope of the problem. Others are purely speculative. The rule that unknown facts are to be assumed both ways is not just a law school technique. In writing a memorandum for a senior lawyer you might have to complete the memorandum without being able to determine some relevant fact. For the guidance of the reader you would indicate your opinion on alternative facts. Again, a judge might decide a case and refer it to an official (often the Master) to determine an unknown fact, indicating in advance what disposition is to follow each possible factual determination.

PROBLEMS IN SEVERAL PARTS

Where a problem contains two parts, both must be dealt with, even if your conclusion on the first point makes the second irrelevant. Consider this example:

> A advertises in a newspaper a reward of $50.00 for the return of his lost wallet. B, who never reads newspapers, finds the wallet and returns it in consequence of a card bearing A's name and address. A promises to give B $10.00 as a reward, but before he pays, B sees the newspaper advertisement and demands $50.00. Advise A.

The first part of the problem turns on the question of whether, in order to claim a reward, B must have performed the acts in question with the intention of earning it. If B wins on that point, her claim to $10.00

---

5 *The Wagon Mound,* [1961] A.C. 388 (P.C.).

will not arise. But even if you are sure that B can recover the $50.00 the second point should be dealt with. Having reached your conclusion on the first point, continue: "This conclusion should determine the result, but if I am wrong in my conclusion, the question will arise of B's claim to $10.00 promised after the return of the wallet." Proceed to discuss this question as if you had come to the opposite conclusion on the first point. Consider another example:

> A casually says to B over drinks at their club: "I'll sell you my yacht for $100,000", and B replies: "It's a deal." A later refuses to proceed with the transaction, and B, who has invited all her important business associates to go sailing with her, suffers a nervous breakdown.

Plainly, there are two points in the problem: first, contract formation and second, whether B can recover damages for her nervous breakdown. The second point will not arise if there is no contract, but it must be discussed, and discussed fully, whatever your conclusion on the first point. Do not allow your consideration of the second point to be affected by your conclusion on the first. This answer, for instance, confuses the two points:

> The law cannot recognize B's claim in respect of her nervous breakdown since it is too remote, especially where there is no real contract.

In the law school context, the second part of such questions is included because it is intended to be considered and, of course, its inclusion does not carry any implication as to the examiner's view of the proper result of the first point. The same technique is needed outside the law school. Judges will frequently give several reasons for a decision, in case the first meets with disfavour in the Court of Appeal. Counsel in arguing a case may be sure he can win on point one, but he will prepare and argue the other points in case he loses on the first.

CONCEALED ISSUES

Sometimes the point of a question is not glaringly apparent on its face. Consider this example from the law of contracts:

> Able takes tickets for a voyage for himself and his wife on a ship owned by Baker. Mr. and Mrs. Able are both injured when the gangway is carelessly removed by one of the crew. On the face of the tickets is a clause that reads, "Neither Baker nor his servants shall be made liable for any injury whatsoever to the person of any passenger arising from the activities of Baker's servants, whether occasioned or caused by negligence or otherwise, and in this regard it is agreed that Baker contracts as agent for his servants." Discuss.

Many students will jump to the conclusion that this is a question on the validity of disclaimer clauses, and they will consider that a display of knowledge of the cases on disclaimer clauses satisfactorily answers the problem. But there are two other points in the question, both perfectly clear to a careful reader. The first is the personal liability of the negligent crew member. Even if A cannot sue B, can he sue B's negligent employee personally? Can an agreement between A and B protect B's servants? The language in the disclaimer clause, particularly the triple reference to B's servants, should make it quite clear that this issue is to be discussed. There are, then, two potential defendants. There are also two potential plaintiffs. It should be obvious that a discussion is intended of the injuries to Mrs. Able. This discussion, in turn, will require two branches, that is, first, the question of whether Mr. Able can recover in his own name for Mrs. Able's injuries, and, second, whether Mrs. Able can sue in her own right. A little thought, without any special legal knowledge at all, can turn a very poor answer into a first-class one.

QUESTIONS TO WHICH THE ANSWERS ARE UNKNOWN

Never avoid a problem because you do not know the answer. Law teachers often get the impression that a point left unexplored was seen, or half seen, by the student, but glossed over because it seemed too difficult. An analysis is always better for recognizing problems even if the answer is unknown. Often a discussion that any intelligent person could write from first principles will form the foundation of a first-class answer despite gaps in the answerer's knowledge. Suppose, as part of a problem in criminal law, you are told that a robber was shot at by the police, who want to remove a foreign object from A's leg to discover whether it is a police bullet. As a matter of fact there is a case on the point,[6] but you should never avoid the issue because you do not know of it or because you have an idea that there was something in the field but cannot remember what it was. An excellent answer can be written without any knowledge of the case at all. Ask yourself what is the general source of the power of the police to search. The answer is section 487 of the Criminal Code which authorizes the issue of search warrants (you will generally have the Criminal Code available even if you have no other sources of information). Section 487 says a warrant can be issued for the search of a "building, receptacle or place." Is A's leg a place? In one sense, of course, it is, but perhaps not within the meaning of section 487. If Parliament meant to authorize compulsory surgery, it could have made itself much clearer. There is a public interest in efficient police investigation, but also in the physical

---

6 *Re Laporte and The Queen* (1972), 8 C.C.C. (2d) 343 (Que. Q.B.). See above, p. 3.

integrity of the person who is only suspected. Whichever side you come down on, you have the makings of a good discussion of the point. Reference to the decided case would improve the answer, but only slightly. The case does not settle the issue for all time. It could be overruled in a higher court. Even a decision of the Supreme Court of Canada is not unalterable.

ESSAY QUESTIONS

Sometimes you will be asked to write an answer to a question that directly invites your opinion on some matter. If the question raises a controversial issue on which you have strong views, there is a temptation to express only one side of the argument. This may lead to acceptable journalism, but not to a good legal analysis. A useful guide is to start out by putting the argument against your own view as strongly as possible. Imagine yourself in the position of an advocate briefed to argue the case, perhaps before a legislative committee, and put the best case you can. Only then put the other side of the case. By all means conclude by expressing your own view, but do not let it interfere with your appreciation of the strength of the opposing view.

Sometimes you will be asked to comment on a quotation. Consider this question from the law of contracts:

[In the nineteenth century] there seems to have been a hardening of equity's arteries, an increasing technicality until quite recent times. The Chancellor's foot evolves into the Vice-Chancellor's footrule. (Lord Simon) Discuss.

The first piece of advice is to read the quotation carefully. Some readers assume that this is a question on the history of equity, and write all they know about that subject. It should be obvious that the question is about flexibility and rigidity in judicial decision making. Every law student knows about the Chancellor's foot (justice was said to vary according to the length of the Chancellor's foot; that is, unrestricted discretion led to arbitrary and uncertain decisions). The Vice-Chancellor's footrule is a new idea, but the meaning of the metaphor again should be obvious in the light of the whole quotation. From the evils of unstructured discretion the pendulum swings over to the opposite side and gives us the evils of mechanical and inflexible decision-making (the "footrule").

Having perceived the general meaning of the quotation, you will see what general topic you are invited to discuss, in this case, the comparative advantages and dangers of flexibility and rigidity in judicial decision-making. But there is more to be learned from the quotation. The writer speaks of a "hardening of equity's arteries" and of "increasing technicality". These are not terms of approbation. If you like what the courts have been doing, you do not call it "technicality", you call it stability, predictability, certainty and the rule of law. So it can be deduced that Lord Simon is expressing a criticism of what he sees as an undue rigidity since the nineteenth century. There is a further point to be gleaned from the quotation. Lord Simon says "until quite recent times". He thereby implies that rigidity is now giving way to greater flexibility and that the pendulum is beginning to swing back to a pre-nineteenth century view of the legal system. You are invited to discuss these historical trends. This line of thinking will undoubtedly furnish you with ample illustrations, and provides the framework for a first-class answer.

UNCONVENTIONAL ANALYSIS

You may have strong views on a legal point that are derived from former fields of study, or from your own social and political views. These views need not be suppressed in your analysis of a legal problem, but care is needed in handling them.

Expert knowledge from another field of study must be transcribed into arguments comprehensible by a non-expert, and it should not displace conventional legal analysis. The best plan is to add the unconventional analysis after the conventional legal analysis is complete. Consider this answer to the case of the stolen watch sold to a good-faith buyer:

> Economic efficiency demands the minimization of transaction costs, and the imposition of liability on the least cost avoider, so in an economic model establishing appropriate parameters and postulating complete availability of information, the buyer must always win, as was shown in 1965 by Zingenblatt and Schillingslott in their noted Chicago study.

It need hardly be said that even if this had any meaning, it is insulting to the reader and useless as a legal analysis. Here is an acceptable way of including an economic view. After a full conventional legal analysis and assessment, add:

> The value just described as "stability of transactions" supports what economists call minimization of transaction costs. The cost of assuring himself of title is a cost that falls on the buyer of goods, and the more readily the law imports a defect in title of goods, the heavier is the cost to the buyer of assuring himself of good title. Against this it may be said that buyers will not actually spend time or money in investigating title to goods, as such investigation is usually impracticable [recognize possible weaknesses in your argument] but whether he bears this cost by extensive search in an individual case or by insurance or self-insurance against the risk of title defect, the result is, in the long run, the same. These heavier transaction costs will not be borne simply by individual buyers but will ultimately be spread more widely. In any case, every owner of goods is also at some point a buyer of goods also, and stands to benefit in the long run by lower transaction costs. In my view,

therefore, these economic considerations add support to a rule of law favouring the good-faith buyer in the circumstances under discussion.

Social and political views require similar care. Here is a possible answer to the same problem:

> The law of theft is a crude instrument designed to protect the property of the wealthy and to oppress the working classes. In my view, so-called "theft" is a redistribution of wealth from the propertied classes to the workers, and is always praiseworthy. Consequently, I do not recognize that the "theft" of goods has any significance at all, so the original so-called owner should not be enabled to recover the goods.

Again, it should be plain that this will not do as a legal analysis. Even though you hope to see the law of property and of theft abolished, as a law student you must discuss the problem on the assumption that those laws will continue to exist, at least for a time. You should take the view that the best ultimate solution may be abolition of private property but that meanwhile there is a case for rational analysis and discussion of the existing law.

Here is an acceptable way of introducing such views. After a full legal discussion and conventional analysis of the problem add:

> Stability of ownership is a concept particularly likely to appeal to property owners. It is relevant to point out that eighteenth and nineteenth-century judges, on the whole, were drawn from property-owning classes of society, and the favour they have given to the owner's position may perhaps be explained on this basis. On the other hand, it may be said that the dispute in the case discussed is not a dispute between property owner and indigent but one between two property owners, or, rather, two competing claimants, both of whom wish to be property owners [recognize weaknesses in your argument]. Nevertheless, in my view, the background of the judges may well have made them more willing to support the position of the property owner, and "stability of ownership" in a society is always beneficial to those in it who themselves enjoy a large measure of that ownership and are reasonably satisfied with the status quo. This may not be so true in Canada today, where judges are drawn as much from commercial and business classes as from "propertied" classes in the traditional European sense. Canadian judges are drawn from the "bourgeoisie" rather than from the "aristocracy" of European political analysis. Commercial transactions are the source of most of the wealth of the bourgeoisie. It would not be surprising, therefore, to see among modern judges signs of sympathy with the position of a good-faith buyer, and support for "stability of transactions".

Sometimes a student is too much influenced by the conclusions of his own law school instructors. Law teachers are occasionally tempted to express a cynical view of the legal process and to assume an attitude of intellectual superiority towards judges. The wise student will take such attitudes with a grain of salt. The student is not excused from learning the law herself because her instructor (rightly or wrongly) takes a cynical attitude to it. Consider this answer to the problem of sale by a non-owner:

> There are plenty of cases supporting the original owner, and plenty more supporting the good-faith buyer. The truth is that these cases are not reconcilable. The court in each case makes the findings appropriate to the conclusion it desires to reach. The result, therefore, will depend simply on which party attracts the sympathy of the judge.

The writer's conclusion here (that the cases are not reconcilable) may well be supportable, but it must follow, and not be substituted for, the writer's own analysis of the conflicting cases.

Again, it is a perfectly tenable position that the law should not recognize such an instrument as a will. It is not immediately apparent that those who have chosen not to give their property away during their life should enjoy the privilege, if such it be, of doing so after their death, thereby involving those left behind them in a great deal of uncertainty, confusion and expense. But not every question on the law of wills can be treated as an invitation to expound this thesis. For a few years, at any rate, the law of wills is likely to survive and the law student cannot excuse himself from learning it by a sudden conversion to an abolitionist viewpoint.

LEGAL RESEARCH AND WRITING

Some law schools teach "legal writing" as a subject separate from any branch of substantive law. Others combine instruction in legal writing with one or more of the substantive courses. Legal writing cannot exist in a void, and good legal writing is writing that is effective for its purpose. If you are asked to analyze a legal problem, the analysis should be approached along the lines suggested in this chapter, whatever the invited format of the analysis. A case comment invites a critical examination of a court's analysis of a legal problem. A useful approach is to examine the prior state of the law, assess the change made by the new case, discuss the reasons given by the court and conclude with your own views of the merits of the decision. The three questions included at the end of the case brief on page 28 above, would provide the basis for a critical analysis of *Jarvis v. Swans Tours*, and should be discussed in a comment on that case. Exercises in statutory or contractual drafting require clear thinking and accurate use of language. If, as is common, you are invited to give notes on your draft you will require the same kind of analysis as has been discussed in this chapter in order to weigh conflicting arguments on the prior state of the law and the effect of your draft.

Legal research is not something that can be taught in the abstract. All law students learn at an early stage how to find their way around a law library. Good legal research is a matter of finding what is relevant for the writer's particular purpose. In analyzing a legal problem you will look for any applicable statutes or regulations, and then for relevant Canadian and Commonwealth cases, and, particularly if there is an absence of Canadian and Commonwealth cases, for American cases. Subsequent references to decided cases can be found by use of the Dominion Law Reports Annotation Service (for Canadian cases), the Index to the Law Reports (for English cases) and Shepard's Citations (for American cases). Textbooks and articles in periodicals will often be useful. There is an excellent Index to Legal Periodicals, covering American and Commonwealth periodicals. There is also an Index to Canadian Legal Literature. Textbooks and articles will often be a convenient source of reference to important decided cases in the area of your interest, and cases themselves refer to previously decided cases. Digests, encyclopedias and abridgments will give references to further cases. In specialized fields there are looseleaf services which provide up-to-date accounts of all statutes, regulations and decisions in their respective fields. The main Canadian, English and American digests and encyclopedias, and the principal Canadian looseleaf services, are listed in Appendix C.

Computers are of increasing importance to legal research. Computer programs are in use that will reveal all cases in which certain words, or combinations of words, appear.

EXAMINATIONS

Most of the advice given in this chapter about analyzing legal problems applies to examination answers. Here are some additional pieces of advice. Always ration your time carefully according to the marks allocated to each question. Spend about half the time allotted to each question in thinking and making notes. Make a written note of every point as soon as it occurs to you. Always show your rough notes in the answer book to indicate to the examiner that you have considered the structure of the answer, and in case you should accidentally omit a point later. You will almost never lose by thinking out your answer, because if you run out of time you can, if necessary, complete the answer in note form, from which the examiner will see that you had the structure of the answer fully worked out and were quite capable of completing it with sufficient time. If, on the other hand, you start writing too soon, there is a real danger of overlooking important aspects of the question, of jumping too soon to a conclusion, and of bad organization of your answer. Actually, you will find that you will rarely run out of time if you spend half your time thinking, because a well considered answer can be written far more quickly than one not thought through in advance.

5

PUBLIC LAW

CRIMINAL LAW

The criminal law is generally sharply distinguished from civil or private law. A single act, for example an assault, may constitute at the same time both a crime and a civil wrong (tort), but the proceedings and their results are very different. Suppose that Smith beats Jones on the head and injures him. Both criminal and civil proceedings may ensue. Criminal proceedings take place before a criminal court, that is, a provincially or federally appointed judge with or without a jury. The case is brought in the name of the Queen as representing the State, and its title will be *Regina v. Smith.* A Crown prosecutor will organize and argue the case for the Crown. Smith will be asked whether she "pleads" "guilty" or "not guilty". Jones will usually appear as a witness for the Crown, but he has no personal control over the proceedings, cannot discontinue them even if he wants to, and usually gets no personal benefit from them. The result, on proof of guilt beyond a reasonable doubt, will be a sentence passed on Smith of a fine or imprisonment. The fine will go not to Jones but into the coffers of the State.

On the other hand, if Jones brings a civil action against Smith it will be instituted in a court of civil jurisdiction, variously named in different provinces. Jones issues a statement of claim. Smith enters a defence. Jones must brief his own lawyer, has complete control over the proceedings, may settle them or discontinue them whenever he likes, must prove his case on the balance of probabilities, and recovers money for himself if he is successful.

In many cases of criminal assault, a civil action against the wrongdoer proves to be ineffective as a means of securing compensation for the person injured. This is because often the offender is not possessed of sufficient resources to make a civil action worthwhile. To deal with such cases, the provinces have established Criminal Injuries Compensation Boards, which pay monetary compensation out of State funds to those injured by criminal offences. On making a payment, the Board then may exercise, for the benefit of public funds, any right of civil action that the victim may have had against the wrongdoer. In her claim against the Compensation Board, Jones has to deal with the State as administrator and regulator. Her claim, and the proceedings that govern it, are part of what is called Administrative Law.

The different considerations that affect criminal and civil proceedings were vividly illustrated by a CBC television series shown in about 1960.[1] The facts of the case in question were that a hunter shot at something he saw moving in the bush, not able to see it distinctly, but thinking it to be a deer. In fact it was a man who was hit and seriously wounded. The hunter was charged with criminal negligence, and was also sued civilly by the victim of the accident. In the course of the criminal proceedings it transpired that the victim was a beater employed to assist the hunting party, who was deliberately taking a short-cut, contrary to instructions, across the line of fire. Moreover, he was not wearing the bright red hat with which he was equipped for the very purpose of avoiding such an accident as in fact occurred. None of this was held to be relevant to the criminal charge. The safety of the community requires hunters never to discharge guns at moving objects that cannot be clearly distinguished. So far as the hunter's criminal liability was concerned, it was irrelevant that the victim happened to have been negligent. It might equally have been an entirely innocent person who had no connection with the hunting expedition. The focus of the proceedings is on the conduct of the accused,not on the merits of the victim. A criminal conviction can be justified even when no injury is caused to anyone.

On the other hand, when it comes to the civil action, the victim's negligence is very relevant. The focus shifts from control of the hunter's conduct in the interests of society to the merits of compelling the hunter to compensate the victim's loss. This loss is only partly caused by the hunter; a contributory cause is the negligent conduct of the victim himself. In the result the hunter was held liable to pay only half the victim's loss.

The division between criminal and civil law is reflected in different language used for the two kinds of proceedings. Criminal proceedings are called prosecution, and Smith will be called the accused. An adverse finding is a conviction. In civil proceedings, Jones sues, or brings an action against Smith. Jones is the plaintiff, and Smith the defendant. Smith will be found liable and Jones will recover judgment. The linguistic and procedural distinctions correspond to an important distinction of substance. In a civil

---

1 The series was called "A Case for the Court".

case the plaintiff has as much right to a judgment, if his case is meritorious, as the defendant has to a dismissal of the action if it is unmeritorious. So if the plaintiff proves that, on balance, his case is the better, he has a right to succeed. But in a criminal case the victim of an assault is not a party to the proceedings and has no "right" to a conviction of the assailant. If anyone can be said to have a right to a conviction, it is the Crown, representing the whole community. On this basis rest the very important principles that the accused in a criminal case is entitled to the benefit of any reasonable doubt and to protection from procedures that might be seen as unfair. It has always been thought better that nine guilty persons should go free than that one innocent should be convicted, for the consequences of a wrongful conviction of serious crime (in contrast to the wrongful imposition of civil liability) are quite horrifying; moreover the cost of the error is paid by a single person, whereas the cost of a wrongful acquittal is spread over the community. The origins of criminal and civil law, however, are not distinct, and certain terms are sometimes interchanged. An accused is often called the defendant. One speaks of criminal defences, and of criminal liability. On the other hand, old tort cases include the plea of not guilty. A civil action can be dismissed for want of prosecution.

In substance, too, the distinction is not quite as watertight as theory might suggest. A plaintiff in a tort action can recover exemplary damages, that is, damages that go beyond compensation, in order to punish the defendant. Criminal courts can make orders of restitution directing the offender to make payment to the victim of a crime, often as a condition of probation.

Several voices have recently been heard advocating the extension of the practice of restitution orders by criminal courts. Others, however, have sounded a note of caution. In favour of restitution orders it is argued that it is sensible to determine all the issues in a single proceeding, that the victim is "the forgotten person" in the criminal process, and should recoup some personal benefit from the proceedings, and making a direct payment to his victim will bring home to the offender the effect on the victim of the offence and is likely to inculcate a greater sense of responsibility in the offender. Against these arguments must be set the fear that the court will use the coercive powers of criminal punishment to extort a settlement for the benefit of private persons. The proper measure of compensation may bear no relation to the culpability of the offender's conduct. Dangerous driving is an obvious example; a comparatively venial oversight may inflict very serious injuries. Is it desirable for the court that has to assess the appropriate punishment for the offender's conduct also to take into account the question of compensation for the victim? We long ago abolished debtor's prison. Is there, perhaps, a danger of bringing it back in another form if we invite the court to make restitution orders enforced by threat of criminal sanctions? Where the same judge determines guilt and compensates the victim, is there not a danger that sympathy for the victim and the desire to secure compensation for her might affect the initial finding of guilt? Further, it may be argued, combining the proceedings will not, in point of fact, save much time if both sets of proceedings are properly pursued. Ordinarily, in a criminal prosecution, the Crown does not have to prove the exact extent of the victim's injuries. If an accused person is charged with theft from his employer, the exact amount that he has stolen, assuming it to be over $1,000,[2] is irrelevant to the finding of guilt. If, however, the criminal court is charged with the duty of making compensation to the victim, it must develop procedures for the proof of the exact amount that the victim claims to have lost, and the accused should have the right to demand strict proof of the amount claimed. Criminal proceedings are not at present adapted to this purpose, and if they were so adapted, they would be considerably lengthened. Perhaps, after all, there is something to be said for the traditional system of separating the proof and punishment of guilt from the question of injury compensation.

Crimes were formerly divided into treason, felonies, and misdemeanours, and these terms are still in current American usage. In Canada, however, the more serious offences are called indictable (all of which formerly were, and some of which still are triable by judge and jury) and the less serious are summary offences (triable by magistrate or judge alone). A wide range of offences can be treated as indictable or summary at the option of the Crown.

ADMINISTRATIVE LAW

The relationship between the individual and the State is not exhausted by the criminal law. The modern State has enormously important regulatory functions, and the relationship between the individual and the State as regulator is the concern of administrative law. An administrative decision in a highly regulated State can have a much greater effect on an individual than a criminal disposition. For example, removal of an offender's driving licence may have far more drastic consequences than a fine or even a short period of imprisonment. Any description of law-making institutions must take account not only of the legislatures and the courts but of the thousands of administrative and regulatory tribunals.

The example was given above of a claim by a victim of a criminal assault against the Criminal Injuries Compensation Board. How is the claim

---

2 Section 334 of the Criminal Code distinguishes between theft over $1,000, punishable by ten years' imprisonment, and theft under $1,000, punishable by two years' imprisonment.

to be regarded? Is the Board a welfare agency that simply dispenses benefits as a matter of grace? Or can we regard the claimant as having a "right" to the benefits? If she has a right, what procedures are appropriate to enforce it? Is the claimant entitled to appear before the Board, to bring her own witnesses to tell the Board what the facts of the case were, to hear the witnesses on whom the Board relies, to cross-examine them and to know the facts on which the Board might draw a conclusion adverse to the claimant? What happens when an adverse decision is made? Has the claimant an appeal to some other tribunal or body? Can she go to the court with a complaint that the Board has drawn erroneous conclusions of fact, or has erroneously decided that the claim is invalid? These questions are the concern of administrative law, and in the welfare State, it is obvious that they are becoming of more and more importance.

Every law school curriculum includes a general course in Administrative Law, and a variety of courses that may be regarded as specialized aspects of the subject, such as Labour Law, Land Use Control, Protection of the Environment, Economic Regulation, Communications Law, etc.

CONSTITUTIONAL LAW

Constitutional law assumes an importance in Canada greater than in most other federal countries. This is because the relationship between governments in Canada is still in a state of flux. Consequently, many questions of jurisdiction are disputed that in other federal States have long ago been settled, and every constitutional decision is an important political matter when it affects the balance of power between the provincial and federal governments. To an American lawyer, constitutional law consists largely of the Bill of Rights, the Americans having generally settled the primacy of Congress. American constitutional law is by and large part of the balance of interests between the individual and the State. So it is also in England where constitutional law is generally taken to include the relationship of the State with the individual. The establishment, in 1982, of a Charter of Rights in the Canadian constitution has introduced these matters into Canadian constitutional law.

But, in Canada, unlike England and the United States, the basic structure of the State is far from settled. Indeed, the future of Confederation is in doubt, and insofar as the legal system can, as on occasion it must, deal with the problems of intergovernmental relations, these are the concern of constitutional law. The Supreme Court of Canada is thus compelled to play a political role. The allocation of powers between the federal and provincial levels of government cannot be determined on the basis simply of reason applied to agreed general principles. One of the reasons for the continuing debate and dissatisfaction about the constitution of the Supreme

Court of Canada itself is the dual role that it has to play as both the final adjudicator of disputes to be settled on generally accepted legal principles and the final arbiter of the powers of the federal and provincial levels of government in Canada.[3]

INTERNATIONAL LAW

Law on the international stage is something rather different. Public international law is taught in most university law schools, and has always been regarded as part of the study of law. Some would dispute whether it is properly called law, or at least whether it is law in the same sense as domestic law or municipal law (the names given by international lawyers to the internal law of States). Domestic law depends ultimately on an effective means of enforcement. This is lacking in international law. A discussion, for example, of whether or not war is illegal has a certain unreality when one of the prospective participants is a great power. It has been said of international law that "as understood by traditionalists it appears to be obsolete, and as understood by modernists it appears to be premature."[4]

On the other hand, international lawyers point out that undoubted rules of domestic law are often not observed or enforced, while many rules of international law are generally followed, and that principles of international law are commonly invoked to justify the conduct of States. No one would deny that some patterns of predictable and civilized behaviour can be detected in the dealings of States with each other, and it is plainly in the interests of all of us to recognize and encourage them.

---

3 See below, pp. 109-114, for further comments on the Supreme Court of Canada.
4 Quincy Wright, quoted by E.B. Wang in a lecture at Trinity College, Toronto, March 16, 1981.

6

PRIVATE LAW

DIVISIONS OF PRIVATE LAW

The chief branches of substantive private law are Contracts, Torts, Restitution and Property. A first-year curriculum in a Canadian law school will generally include courses in Criminal Law, Contracts, Torts, Property and Civil Procedure.

CONTRACTS

The law of contracts is concerned with expectations induced by the conduct of others. Generally, such expectations are induced by promises and, as the name contracts suggests, by agreements. But actions and statements that give rise to expectations are also of concern to the law of contracts.

A study of contract law includes enforceability, excuses for non-performance, remedies, and the effect of contracts on third parties.

Every system of contract law must develop a criterion of enforceability. In Anglo-Canadian law the chief criterion of enforceability has been the bargain, an agreed exchange, and every contracts course will devote attention to the constituent parts of a bargain. There are other reasons for enforcement, or partial enforcement, besides the existence of bargain, in particular, subsequent reliance on a promise.

The chief excuses for non-performance of contracts are mistake, unfairness, public policy, and non-performance by the other party. The courts, since the nineteenth century, have been reluctant to allow a large scope to defences of mistake, unfairness and public policy, chiefly because they feared that a broad power to relieve on these grounds might endanger the stability and predictability that they saw as the chief values of contract law. From one point of view a contract entered into by mistake must be an unjust contract; yet if every mistake were a ground of relief no bargain would be enforceable, for no one willingly makes a bad bargain. In recent years a more flexible attitude has become apparent. The law of contracts involves a continuous tension between stability, certainty and predictability, on the one hand, and fairness, equity and justice in the individual case on the other. A study of changing attitudes to the judicial function forms an interesting and important part of most courses in contract law.

Remedies are a large part of contract law, for no legal right can be defined or understood without an appreciation of its enforceability. Contract formation is closely linked with remedies for breach, for it is only where the remedy seems appropriate that a contract will be found to exist in the first place. The court gives two kinds of remedies for breach of contract, specific and monetary. Specific remedies include a decree of specific performance ordering the defendant to perform her promises, and an injunction ordering the defendant to refrain from doing what she promised not to do. Monetary remedies, usually damages, aim at compensating the plaintiff by measuring her loss in money. The usual measure in contract cases is the sum of money that will put the plaintiff in as good a position as she would have been in had the contract been performed. The result is to secure protection of the plaintiff's expectation, and the measure of damages is often said to protect the plaintiff's expectation interest, in contrast to tort law, where the usual measure is the plaintiff's out-of-pocket loss.

Third-party problems in contract law include the position of the third-party beneficiary of a contract between two others. Related third-party problems include the power of one person to act on behalf of another (agency) and the transfer of contractual rights (assignment).

TORTS

The law of torts, or civil wrongs, formerly thought of as sharply distinguishable from contracts, is now seen to be closely intertwined. Assaults and negligent injuries are torts that can easily be distinguished from contracts. But a negligent statement inducing reliance is very much on the borderline, and the development of the law in this area has led some writers to look forward to general recognition of a unitary law of obligations. Even in systems where there is a unitary law of obligations, however, such as civil law systems, a working distinction is found in practice to be necessary between the law of contracts and the law of civil wrongs.

One way of approaching the law of torts is to divide the subject according to the defendant's state of mind into intentional wrongs, negligence and strict liability (that is, liability without fault). A second way of approaching the subject is to consider the various interests of the plaintiff that are protected, that is, injury to the person, injury to property, injury to reputation, interference with the use of land, rights of privacy, and interference with economic interests. A third approach is to classify by the activity carried on by the defendant, for example, liability for animals, liability for products, liability of occupiers and owners of property, employer's liability. Generally all three methods of classification are used in law school courses in tort law. A typical course might start with intentional torts, continue with negligence, examine tort law as a means of compensating personal injuries, compare strict liability, consider other possible compensation schemes, then go on to protection of interests in land, rights of privacy, defamation, economic torts, occupiers' liability, employers' liability and products liability.

Intentional torts include assault and battery (damage to the plaintiff's person), trespass to land and trespass to goods, conversion and detinue (remedies for misappropriation of goods).

The law of negligence has expanded greatly in the last fifty years and has provided a means of achieving a somewhat rough and ready scheme of accident compensation. Persons injured by accident are compensated if they can show a solvent defendant to have been at fault. If the defendant is a motorist, a large-scale employer, manufacturer, or a governmental body, the loss will be spread through insurance or otherwise over a sizeable part of the public. There is a noticeable tension in the law of negligence between the need for compensation of accident victims, and a genuine enquiry into the defendant's fault. As an accident compensation system the law of negligence is greatly deficient, for it will compensate only accident victims who can prove that the accident was caused by the fault of a solvent or insured defendant. Moreover, once the main purpose of the system is recognized as compensation it becomes obvious that the litigation system is not only a haphazard but a very expensive system. Would it not be preferable openly to recognize the social desirability of compensating accident victims regardless of fault, and to replace the present scheme with a straightforward compensation scheme? For years Canada has treated workers' compensation in this way and no one seriously suggests a return to the fault system for injured workers. Against a comprehensive accident compensation scheme it is argued that there is merit in the large awards that courts occasionally make to seriously injured persons, and that the courts can perform a useful function in controlling objectionable conduct by giving it publicity, and by making punitive awards of damages, both of which functions might be less effectively performed by an administrative tribunal. Further, there is a fear that a State-run accident compensation scheme might not maintain adequate levels of compensation. Once the principle of full compensation for wrongful injuries is abandoned, there seems no reason to distinguish accident victims from other claimants to social welfare, who may, indeed, be in greater need. New Zealand has adopted a comprehensive accident compensation scheme, and some moves have been made in Canada towards no-fault compensation for victims of automobile accidents. One of the most important questions in tort law is whether we are likely to follow New Zealand in adopting a comprehensive accident compensation scheme.

RESTITUTION

The third branch of the law of obligations is restitution, the branch of the law dealing with unjust enrichment. If I mistakenly pay A $100 thinking she is my creditor B, A is unjustly enriched and must restore the payment. There is no contract broken or wrong committed by A. The liability to repay rests on principles of unjust enrichment. Restitution is closely related to and in some aspects not fully distinguishable from the law of contracts and torts. Curiously enough, restitution is not taught as part of the first-year curriculum in most law schools. There are historical reasons for this. The open recognition of restitution as a separate branch of the law of civil obligations is comparatively recent, and a study of the subject requires considerable knowledge of other areas of the law. Consequently, there are reasons of convenience for reserving it to a later part of the curriculum.

Besides mistake, mentioned above, the main reasons for restitution are that the defendant has benefited from a wrongful act, or from a breach of a relationship of trust, or that the plaintiff has conferred the benefit under compulsion, or in an emergency to save the defendant's life or property.

The relationship of restitution and contracts raises interesting and difficult questions. A benefit conferred by one contracting party on another is generally conferred in anticipation of an exchange performance that is the agreed equivalent. Restitution problems arise when the exchange performance fails to materialize. If the failure to render the exchange performance constitutes an actionable breach of contract, contract law will provide a remedy, though if the benefit conferred exceeds the value of the anticipated exchange the contractual remedy may not satisfy the plaintiff. However, if the contract is unenforceable for some reason, such as public policy, or failure to comply with formalities, or breach of contract by the plaintiff himself, the question will arise of whether the plaintiff is entitled to restitution. To what extent can a right of restitution be reconciled with the policies of contract law that have made the contract unenforceable in the first place? An even more difficult problem arises where the defendant renders the performance promised in exchange for the benefit, but because of some fundamental mistake in the plaintiff's assumptions the performance disappoints him. A spends her life savings to buy land from B for $50,000 for her retirement home. B is willing to convey the land, but it turns out that it has been zoned forever for agricultural use only. No house can be built on it and its value is $500. Is this just an unfortunate case of a bad bargain (in which case contract values prevail and A loses) or is it a case of unjust enrichment (in which case restitution values prevail, and A wins)? There is no easy answer to that question.

PROPERTY

The law of property, as its name suggests, concerns rights over goods and land, including their extent, acquisition and transfer. The law of property is an essential background to the law of civil obligations. It is wrongful to interfere with another's enjoyment of his property. One can bargain freely to sell what is one's own. Thus, the laws of torts and contracts assume the existence of, and are in a sense dependent on, a law of property.

The study of property law is divided into real and personal property. Real property is (broadly speaking) land and interests in land. Personal property includes goods and intangible items of property, such as rights of action and interests in patents, copyright and trademarks.

Real property is the most venerable part of our system of law, and ancient concepts have survived here more than elsewhere. A basic study of property law will examine various interests in land, including joint ownership, leases and future interests. The detailed study of the transfer of interests in land, and land security transactions (mortgages) is generally reserved to a specialized course on real estate transactions.

Specialized aspects of personal property are also usually reserved for specialized courses. Thus, patents, copyrights and trademarks are usually reserved to a course in industrial property. Security interests in goods (pledges, liens, chattel mortgages, conditional sales, personal property security) as well as the law relating to transfer of goods by sale are usually dealt with in courses on commercial law. The first-year course on property will, however, generally include a study of gifts, bailments (lending of goods) and finding.

CIVIL PROCEDURE

The inclusion of civil procedure in the usual first-year curriculum is not intended to turn first-year law students into instant practitioners. The reason for its inclusion is that substantive law and procedure are inextricably intertwined. A legal right is not worth having, indeed it is not worthy of the name, unless an effective procedure exists for enforcing it. And a legal right is only worth just so much as can be effectively enforced.

As Professor Karl Llewellyn wrote: "Procedural regulations are the door, and the only door, to make real what is laid down by substantive law."[1]

An example of the influence of procedure on substantive rights is the question of the right to bring an action against a defendant who is outside the jurisdiction. Suppose that a person in Saskatchewan is electrocuted by a defective light fixture manufactured in Ontario. The right of the Saskatchewan plaintiff to sue the Ontario manufacturer in Saskatchewan will depend on the Saskatchewan rule of practice. The rules vary from province to province. In Saskatchewan an action in tort against an out-of-province defendant can be instituted if the tort is committed in Saskatchewan. Many people would say that manufacture of a light fixture in Ontario is not the commission of a tort in Saskatchewan, and several cases had said so, but in 1974 the Supreme Court of Canada held that if the manufacturer could foresee that its products would go into Saskatchewan, it was to be treated, for the purposes of the rule, as though it had committed the tort in Saskatchewan.[2] It is obvious that the interpretation and operation of the rule is not a purely procedural matter, but vitally affects the plaintiff's rights. The policy behind the decision of the Supreme Court was plainly that a manufacturer who makes a profit from the Saskatchewan market must be prepared to go there to answer when its products turn out to be defective. It should perhaps be added that even if the plaintiff is successful, the judgment will be valueless unless the defendant has assets in Saskatchewan, or unless the judgment is enforceable in Ontario. This last possibility will depend on Ontario law. It is always important to remember that a judgment is not self-executing, and will be useless if the defendant does not have assets available to satisfy it.

GENERAL FIRST-YEAR COURSES

Many law schools have in recent years experimented with variations on the theme of a general introductory course for first-year students. These have had only mixed success, partly because they have an uncertain focus and attempt to achieve a variety of different purposes. The purposes generally mentioned are to give some sort of introduction to legislation, and particularly to regulation, the latter being a vital part of the modern State on which little emphasis is traditionally placed in the common law first-year courses. The relationship between the individual and the State as regulator is as important a part of public law as criminal law itself. The designers of the general first-year courses also aim at including an introduction to legal institutions and legal reasoning, something on

---

1 Llewellyn, *The Bramble Bush* (1960 ed.), p. 17.
2 *Moran v. Pyle Nat. (Can.) Ltd.,* [1975] S.C.R. 393.

interpretation of statutes, *stare decisis*, and the relationship of the courts to other institutions. Parts of the course generally have a jurisprudential slant. Often some legal history and informational material on the Canadian legal system is included, together with the organization of the legal profession, and legal ethics. Sometimes there is practical information on methods of legal research and using a law library. Some law schools have also attempted to involve practising lawyers to give an understanding of the practice of law, and to include legal writing (either of an academic or of a practical variety in case comments and draft pleadings).

It will be seen that such a variety of unrelated, and even in part conflicting, objectives is a very heavy burden to place on a single course. To make matters worse, many law schools have found an absence of enthusiasm among their faculty for the privilege of teaching such courses. The result is that the course is often taught by reluctant instructors sometimes assisted by busy practitioners with no real commitment to the course or understanding or sympathy with its objectives. It is not surprising that such courses have often run into difficulties. There is something to be said for following the traditional method of allowing first-year law students to acquire knowledge of at least some of the matters mentioned above interstitially, as they need it for understanding legal problems in other courses. The danger, of course, of this approach is that important gaps may remain unfilled.

QUEBEC LAW

Quebec, like many countries throughout the world, has a system based on Roman law. Federal statutes operate in Quebec, so that criminal law, and certain aspects of commercial law such as bankruptcy and bills of exchange are governed by the same law as prevails elsewhere in Canada. But the whole law of civil obligations, property and family law (except divorce) is based on the Civil Code, which is derived from the Code Napoleon. The principle of liability for damage caused by negligence developed by the common law through hundreds of judicial decisions, is contained in a single article:

> 1053. Every person capable of discerning right from wrong is responsible for the damage caused by his fault to another, whether by positive act, imprudence, neglect or want of skill.

From one point of view a Quebec judge has less discretion than her common law counterpart, for she is bound by a specific provision. From another point of view she has far more flexibility, for the language of the provision is so general as to leave the difficult questions in the hands of the individual judges. In theory, judicial decisions do not make law; they are simply applications of the unchanging provisions of the Code. In practice, however, the law, even in a codified system, is able to develop to meet changing social needs, and a civil law judge is aware of the interpretation currently being given by the courts to provisions of the Code. Judicial decisions, therefore, are not so unimportant as pure theory would suggest.

Comparing two systems of law is a difficult task. All systems of law make use of fictions, and the rules to which they pay lip service are not always what they seem. Often a comparison of two systems will reveal diametrically opposed rules in theory, but similar results in nine out of ten actual cases. Comparative law is not included in every law school curriculum, but it is hard to disagree with the view that in Canada especially, with its two systems of law, a course on the Quebec civil law should be offered in every law school.

OTHER SUBJECTS

In addition to the subjects mentioned so far, all Canadian law schools offer courses in Evidence, Taxation, Agency, Company Law, Sale of Goods, Negotiable Instruments, Chattel Security, Debtor and Creditor, Family Law, Insurance, Wills and Trusts, Jurisprudence, Real Estate Transactions, and a variety of other subjects. These courses are not always known by the names given and are not always offered as separate courses. A very important part of the private law that is often neglected in summary descriptions is the area of law governing the effect of foreign elements in a dispute. This is the branch of law generally known as Conflict of Laws, also sometimes called Private International Law. Courts will not take jurisdiction over all disputes everywhere; when they take jurisdiction they may be faced with the problem of whether to apply their own law or the law of some other jurisdiction with which the dispute is connected. These questions (jurisdiction and choice of law) together with the problems of enforcement of foreign judgments, are the main components of Conflict of Laws.

This catalogue of courses would be common to all the common law schools, but it gives no sense of the variety of the various curriculums. Many schools include an extensive list of optional subjects, varying from time to time with the interests of available instructors. Several schools have multidisciplinary programmes in conjunction with other divisions of the university. Areas that particularly lend themselves to such treatment include economics, criminology, social welfare and environmental control. No doubt further areas of multidisciplinary interest will appear in the future.

7

THE COMMON LAW

MEANING OF "COMMON LAW"

Just as "civil law" has a variety of meanings, according to the subject with which it is contrasted,[1] so also does the phrase "common law". One common meaning of the expression is a system of law based primarily on judicial decisions as contrasted with a system based on Roman law, (usually, but not always, based on a Code). Thus, we speak of Quebec and Louisiana and Scotland as civil law jurisdictions (their systems being based on Roman law) and of the other eleven Canadian provinces and territories, the other American states, England, New Zealand, and Australia as common law jurisdictions.

Internally, within a common law legal system, the phrase "common law" has two separate meanings, each quite distinct from that just mentioned. Before the late nineteenth century (1881 in Ontario) there were two separate systems of courts: the courts of law, or common law, on the one hand, and equity on the other. The distinction is still important for some purposes and will be discussed in the next chapter. A third meaning of common law is that area of the law still largely dependent on judicial decisions, as opposed to areas of the law governed mostly by statute. Thus, one can call contracts and torts common law subjects in a sense that income tax is not. Similarly, one could say: "At common law, dandelions could lawfully be planted by anyone, but since the enactment of the Weed Control Act dandelion growers require a licence from the Minister." This chapter is concerned with the common law chiefly in this last sense, that is, as contrasted with statute law.

---

1 See above, note 33, p. 16.

JUDICIAL REASONING

Judicial reasoning is often result-orientated. This comes as a shock to many beginning law students, who assume that judicial conclusions are reached by logical progression. Consider a legal test based on the attributes of the reasonable person (this excellent but odious character, as A.P. Herbert called him, vainly appealing to his fellow citizens to order their lives after his example[2]). A judge has said that a carrier of a mill shaft cannot reasonably foresee that the mill will be stopped if he delays in delivering the mill shaft, so he is not liable for that loss.[3] On the other hand, other judges have said that the seller of defective machinery can reasonably foresee that it is likely to cause injury to persons using it, damage to the user's property, and financial loss. So the seller is usually held liable for those losses. How does the judge know that the carrier cannot foresee the damage, whereas the seller can? Not by any empirical survey of carriers and sellers. The fact is that the judge does not and cannot separate the reason from the result. As one judge said, the reasonable person is but "the anthropomorphic conception of justice."[4] The judge attributes to the reasonable person just those qualities and just that degree of knowledge and foresight that will lead to a result the judge considers desirable. The judge will say that the reasonable seller can foresee injury, therefore, liability follows. But in truth the conclusion does not follow from the reason. The conclusion is hidden in the reason itself, for by holding that the loss is foreseeable the judge has made the conclusion inevitable. The judge does not investigate the degree of foresight in ignorance of the consequences of his finding on that point, as though he could be surprised a moment later to find that it had led him to impose liability. He holds that the seller can foresee the loss because he thinks it right that the seller should be made liable.

Consider another less obvious example. In dealing with contract formation a judge will apparently look at the facts and conclude that there is a contract between A and B. Then she will seem to go on to consider whether A is liable for breach of contract, and, lastly, she will consider what remedy B is entitled to. But the initial question of contract formation is intimately tied in with the question of remedies. The judge will only find that there is a contract in step 1 of her reasoning if she thinks it right that B should have those remedies against A that will follow on such a finding. Consequently, it is futile to discuss contract formation in isolation from remedies. The cases on formation can only be understood by

---

2 A.P. Herbert, *Uncommon Law*, (1959 ed.), p. 4. *Fardell v. Potts; the reasonable man.*

3 *Hadley v. Baxendale* (1854), 9 Exch. 341.

4 Lord Radcliffe in *Davis Contractors Ltd. v. Fareham Urban Dist. Council*, [1956] A.C. 696 at 728 (H.L.).

appreciating that when the judge says "Is this an offer?" what she is really asking is "Is it right and just for B to have the remedy against A that he will have if I should find this to be an offer?" It is absurd to suppose that a judicially reached conclusion can ever be unexpected. The conclusion is always in the judge's mind as she sets out on her path of giving her reasons.

Some law students are distressed to find that judicial reasons generally conceal conclusions. It seems perhaps that the judges are guilty of some kind of deception. In my own view, result-orientated reasoning is inevitable, and indeed desirable. Judges cannot become mere automata drawing in facts and dispensing inevitable conclusions. For the same reason they cannot be replaced by computers. The settlement of human disputes is a human process, and it is fortunate that it cannot be automated. The fact that the reasoning of judges is open to critical analysis does not imply that their decisions are perverse or arbitrary. It is no easy task to explain a decision, as anyone knows who has tried to do it. Moreover, critical analysis of past decisions is as often a technique of arguing for future development of the law as a genuine assessment of the decision. Criticism of former decisions is essential to the flexibility of the common law.

LOGIC, REASON AND THE LAW

Lord Coke claimed that "Reason is the life of the law, nay, the common law itself is nothing else but Reason."[5] Yet the processes of legal reasoning would rarely satisfy a logician. Holmes, a great American judge, wrote that the life of the law has been not logic, it has been experience,[6] and Lord Halsbury, an English judge, said that the law is not always logical.[7] In a recent case the House of Lords had to determine the extent to which drunkenness should be a defence in criminal cases. A general requirement of criminal liability is guilty intent (usually called *mens rea*). If a person is too drunk to know what she is doing how can she have the necessary intention to be convicted of the crime? Logic seems to demand her acquittal of anything more serious than being drunk. Logical though this conclusion is, its adoption would be exceedingly inconvenient for the administration of the criminal law. Drunkenness would confer a virtual immunity from criminal prosecution. Many dangerous offenders would have to be acquitted

---

5 Co. Litt. 97b.

6 Holmes, *The Common Law* (1881), p. 1.

7 "[A] case is only an authority for what it actually decides. I entirely deny that it can be quoted for a proposition that may seem to follow logically from it. Such a mode of reasoning assumes that the law is necessarily a logical code, whereas every lawyer must acknowledge that the law is not always logical at all." *Quinn v. Leathem,* [1901] A.C. 495 at 506 (H.L.) *per* Lord Halsbury L.C.

unless sobriety could be proved. If the law were so established offenders would soon ensure that sobriety should be difficult to prove. The House of Lords saw the practical difficulties and rejected the logic. Lord Salmon said: "I accept that there is a degree of illogicality in the rule. . . . Absolute logic in human affairs is an uncertain guide and a very dangerous master. The law is primarily concerned with human affairs."[8] Lord Edmund-Davies said: "If logic is to be the sole guide, it follows that a man can never be regarded as committing an assault unless he is conscious of what he is doing."[9] Later he quoted a comment made by his fellow law lord, Lord Simon, who had said in the course of argument: "It is all right to say 'Let justice be done though the heavens fall.'[10] But you ask us to say 'Let logic be done even though public order be threatened,' which is something very different."[11] Lord Edmund-Davies added: "If [acquittal of the drunk] be the inescapable result of the strict application of logic in this branch of the law, it is indeed not surprising that illogicality has long reigned, and the prospect of its dethronement must be regarded as alarming."[12]

Other instances of a clash between law and logic come from the law of evidence. Suppose a thousand people enter a football stadium but only four hundred of them buy tickets. It is more probable than not that any one of the entrants has avoided payment. A civil action is decided on the balance of probabilities. Theoretically, therefore, the proprietors of the stadium could sue each of the thousand entrants and win in every case. But plainly this is a theory that a working system of law could never put into practice. Professor Glanville Williams in discussing this example says that the true reason why the proof fails is that it does not sufficiently mark out the defendant from others, adding "No doubt, we are illogical in this."[13]

Another instance where logic and practicality appear to conflict is supplied by the law of causation and damages. Suppose that D tortiously injures P's right foot, causing P to lose his job as a truck driver and to be deprived of ten years' anticipated income. Subsequently before trial, P's right leg has to be amputated for a reason unconnected with D's tort. The question raised by these facts is usually framed by asking whether D's wrong has caused P's loss. Logically it would seem to make no difference to the answer whether the later injury was tortiously caused by a third person or was caused by a pure accident for which no one was responsible, or by disease, pre-existing or subsequently contracted. In the

8 *R. v. Majewski*, [1977] A.C. 443 at 483-4 (H.L.).

9 *Id.* at 487.

10 A translation of the Latin phrase: "fiat justitia, ruat caelum" used by Lord Mansfield in *R. v. Wilkes* (1770), 4 Burr. 2527 at 2562 (H.L.).

11 [1977] A.C. at 494 (H.L.).

12 *Ibid.*

13 "The Mathematics of Proof", [1979] Crim. L.R. 297 at 305.

case where the loss of the leg is purely accidental it seems obvious that D cannot be held responsible for the loss of income after the amputation; that loss would have occurred even if D had not injured P's foot. However, where the loss of the leg is wrongfully caused by a third person, the application of this line of thinking would excuse both wrongdoers. D cannot be liable because the loss would have occurred in any event. The third person cannot be liable because he injured a person who was in any case already incapacitated. This result is intolerable, and so the law, it seems, must accept the illogicality. D's liability is reduced if the subsequent injury is caused otherwise than by a legal wrong; if the subsequent injury is wrongful D remains liable in full.

THE USE OF DECIDED CASES

The principle of reliance on decided cases is called the principle of *stare decisis* (to stand by what has been decided). Some such principle is inevitable if the law is to have stability and continuity. The principle that like cases should be decided alike leads inevitably to records of past cases and an attempt to compare past cases with that to be currently decided.

Not everything a judge says in the course of deciding a case can be binding on her successors, or the common law would have perished long before now from a surfeit of precedents. What is said to be binding is the "decision", but this is an ambiguous concept. The actual facts of the case never arise again in identical form. There are differences in respect of time if in no other respect. As soon as a principle is given for deciding one case that is capable of application to other cases, we have moved from the concrete to a certain level of abstraction. A general rule is given that explains the result in the instant case and will apply to at least some other cases. It is this rule, called the *ratio decidendi* (reason of deciding) that is said to constitute the binding rule for purposes of precedent. Everything else that is said by the judge is called *obiter dicta* (things said by the way). In theory the *ratio decidendi* is binding on lower courts, but the *obiter dicta* are not. In practice, it is an impossible task to isolate the precise ratio and the system of precedent is sufficiently flexible for it to be unnecessary and usually fruitless to attempt too refined an analysis.

Sometimes it is easy to classify judicial statements as *obiter*. Consider the case mentioned earlier of a sale by a non-owner. B steals A's watch and sells it to C. A judge might say: "I find in favour of A because a thief takes no title and can pass none to a purchaser. The result would be the same if B was not a thief but a finder." The comment on finders is *obiter*, and will not bind any subsequent court dealing with a case of a finder. It is an *obiter dictum* because the case of a finder was not before the earlier court. But suppose the judge says:

I decide in favour of A because a thief takes no title and can pass none to a purchaser. In this case A took reasonable care of his watch, but if he had been careless in looking after his watch he would have been precluded from asserting his title against a good-faith buyer.

Here the comment on carelessness is not so clearly *obiter*, because the judge's finding that A was in fact careful is essential to her result. The effect of the comment will depend on the nature of the subsequent case. In a later case of a careful owner, the earlier decision is authoritative in favour of the owner. The principle of the earlier decision could be stated as follows: "A careful owner can assert title to stolen goods against a good-faith buyer from the thief." But if in a subsequent case the owner is found to have been careless, the earlier case will not require a decision either way. The judge's words tend to support a decision in favour of C, the good-faith buyer. But the *ratio* of the case is that the careful owner will win; it is an *obiter dictum* that the careless one will lose.

Often a judge gives two independent reasons for a decision. He might say: "I decide in favour of A because a thief does not obtain title to stolen goods. In any case I find that C knew of A's interest and so she did not buy the watch in good faith and could not assert a title against A, even if B had title to give her." Here either reason would support the result, even if the other were wrong. Is each reason a *ratio decidendi*? Is each *obiter* (because the other would have been sufficient for the result)? Energy spent in seeking an answer to these questions will be wasted. Courts have generally said that in such a case both reasons are binding, but in practice there are several examples of one of two such reasons being treated as *obiter* when a subsequent court is convinced that it is wrong. It was said by the late Professor Llewellyn, a great American law teacher, that every case has to be looked at from two points of view, to determine the narrowest rule that must be conceded by a later hostile court to have been laid down, and to determine the widest rule that a later friendly court could use the earlier case to support.[14]

An analogous case is that of the reason that is wider than necessary for the decision of the case at hand. Suppose A sells his watch to B and takes a cheque that bounces. Meanwhile, B has sold the watch to C, a good-faith purchaser. Primus J. might decide the case in favour of C, on the ground that "whenever one of two innocent persons must suffer by the acts of a third he who has enabled such third person to occasion the loss must sustain it." Suppose in a later case A carelessly leaves his watch in a bus where it is stolen by B who sells it to C. The reason of the earlier case applies to the later. Theoretically, it may be supposed, the later court will be found to apply the earlier case and to decide in favour of C. It

---

14 Llewellyn, *The Bramble Bush* (1960 ed.), p. 68.

is common, however, for the later court to cut down the scope of a wide reason. The court will say that the earlier decision must be considered in the light of its facts. The later court might consider that the earlier judge did not have in mind the possibility of theft, and that the earlier decision should be confined to cases where the owner voluntarily parts with possession. Secunda J.'s judgment might take the following form:

> Primus J.'s reason is far wider than was necessary for the decision of that case. I am sure that he did not intend to reverse the long-established rule that a thief takes and can give no title. Hence, in my own opinion, Primus J.'s principle applies only to cases where the owner parts voluntarily with possession of his goods.

The *ratio decidendi* of the earlier case has in effect been restated: "Where an owner of goods voluntarily parts with possession of them to another, that other can transfer title to a purchaser in good faith."

Further refinements are quite possible. Suppose in the third case, A lends his watch to B who fraudulently sells it to C. Tertius J. could give the following judgment:

> It is important to notice that in case 1 B was a buyer of the watch. Primus J.'s principle only applies, in my opinion, to such cases of contract, or purported contract, and not to a case of simple lending. It is true that in case 2, Secunda J. considered that Primus J.'s principle would apply to any case where the owner voluntarily parts with possession of his goods. However, this dictum is clearly *obiter* since in case 2 Secunda J. decided in favour of the original owner.

In the fourth case, B falsely tells A that he is the Reverend Mr. Chasuble and so induces A to part with possession of the goods. Even the narrowed reason adopted by Tertius J. applies to this case, but it could be still further narrowed, thus: Quarta J.:

> Title in the watch can pass to B, and hence to C, only if there is a valid contract between A and B. Primus J.'s judgment must be read in the light of the facts of case 1, where there was a valid contract. In this case, the mistake of identity makes the contract void. In my opinion, Primus J.'s principle only applies to a case where title is transferred pursuant to a valid contract. It is true that Secunda J. in case 2 thought that a good faith purchaser would be protected whenever the owner had parted voluntarily with possession, and in case 3, Tertius J. thought that any case of "contract or purported contract" would be sufficient to afford protection to the third party purchaser. But these dicta are plainly *obiter*, and I am not bound by them.

By this time, though lip service is paid to the doctrine of *stare decisis* there is very little left of Primus J.'s decision. In fact, as has been pointed out by a number of writers in the field, there is no "true" *ratio decidendi* of a decision. The *ratio decidendi* of a case is only as wide as a subsequent court will concede it to be. This is not to say that the doctrine of *stare decisis* is meaningless. Sometimes a judge will find herself unable to distinguish a former case on any rationally acceptable ground. But the doctrine is a good deal less rigid than it might at first appear.

The technique just described of distinguishing the facts of prior cases is sometimes carried to such lengths that the former case is virtually overruled. Sometimes it is said that a case must be confined to its own special facts. This is equivalent to announcing that it will not be followed, because, of course, the precise facts will never recur.

An example of restrictive distinguishing is available in the field from which other examples have been taken in this book, that is, the sale of goods by a non-owner. In *Ingram v. Little*[15] two elderly ladies, the Misses Ingram, agreed to sell their car to a confidence trickster calling himself P.G.M. Hutchinson. He told a convincing story, and the Ingrams let him take their car in exchange for a cheque. The cheque bounced and the car turned up in the hands of Little, a buyer in good faith. The court held in favour of the Ingrams on the ground that the contract with the rogue was void. So he took no title in the car and could pass none to Little. Eleven years later in *Lewis v. Averay*[16] Lewis sold his car to another rogue calling himself R.A. Green. As in *Ingram v. Little*, the rogue gave a worthless cheque for the car, which was sold to Averay, a good-faith purchaser. Both cases were decided in the English Court of Appeal which considered itself bound by its own previous decisions. It might be thought, then, that Lewis would be certain to win. One judge, Lord Denning, said in *Lewis v. Averay*: "The material facts in each case are quite indistinguishable."[17] But Phillimore L.J. said:

> Now, in that particular case [*Ingram v. Little*] the Court of Appeal, by a majority and in the very special and unusual facts of the case, decided that it had been sufficiently shown in the particular circumstances that, contrary to the prima facie presumption, the lady who was selling the motor car was not dealing with the person actually present. But in the present case I am bound to say that I do not think there was anything which could displace the prima facie presumption that Mr. Lewis was dealing with the gentleman present there in the flat — the rogue.[18]

The third judge, Megaw L.J., said: "For myself, with very great respect, I find it difficult to understand the basis, either in logic or in practical considerations, of the test laid down by the majority of the court in *Ingram v. Little*."[19] It is plain that the court has all but overruled *Ingram v. Little*.

15 [1961] 1 Q.B. 31 (C.A.).
16 [1972] 1 Q.B. 198 (C.A.).
17 *Id.* at 206.
18 *Id.* at 208.
19 *Ibid.*

Note Phillimore L.J.'s references to that "particular" case and to the fact that the decision was "by a majority" and his reference to the "very special" and "unusual" facts of the former case, and to the "particular circumstances" that were "contrary to the prima facie presumption." The court, while paying lip service to the principle that is bound by the earlier case, in reality is refusing to follow it. Phillimore L.J.'s words amount almost to his saying: "The case is different from this case, but I am unable to explain what material distinctions support a different result."

Particular problems arise in attempting to distill a *ratio decidendi* from decisions of appellate courts where there are three, five, seven or nine judges. Suppose the issue of the stolen watch comes before the Supreme Court of Canada sitting with nine judges. B steals A's watch and sells it to C. Three judges hold for A on the ground that a thief can pass no title in stolen goods, even to a good-faith buyer, as they find C to have been. Two judges hold for A on the ground that, although a thief can pass title in stolen goods to a good-faith buyer, on the facts of the particular case C has not acted in good faith. Four judges hold for C on the ground that a thief can pass title to a good-faith buyer and that on the facts C has acted in good faith. There is a majority of five to four for A, who therefore wins. The principle of law, however, that a thief can pass no title, is actually supported by only three judges, and rejected by the other six. Further, a majority of seven judges to two consider that C has acted in good faith. If the two relevant issues were voted on separately, it would be held, by a majority of six to three, that a good-faith buyer from a thief is protected, and by a majority of seven to two that C has acted in good faith. C wins handsomely on each issue, but he will lose the case in the Supreme Court of Canada by a majority of five to four! It would be possible to imagine a case in which, if there were nine separate issues, one party could lose by a vote of eight to one on each issue, and yet have a unanimous decision in his favour!

The doctrine of *stare decisis*, then, is much less restricting in practice than in theory, particularly where appellate courts give multiple judgments. Some writers have expressed the view that single judgments would be desirable for the sake of greater certainty. However, Lord Reid, a Scottish judge, said on this question:

> . . . [My] experience has been that there are dangers in there being only one speech in this House. Then statements in it have often tended to be treated as definitions and it is not the function of a court or of this House to frame definitions: some latitude should be left for future developments. The true ratio of a decision generally appears more clearly from a comparison of two

or more statements in different words which are intended to supplement each other.[20]

A hundred years ago it was commonly believed that legal rules once declared by the court should be unalterable. The courts "declared" the law discovering the answer to every problem in a common law that existed, as a great American judge once said, like a "brooding omnipresence in the sky."[21] Thus the law was to become more and more certain and complete as the judges filled in the gaps, so that eventually there would be a known legal rule for every possible case. This view of the common law has given way to one that recognizes the need for flexibility and change. Lord Reid adopts the more flexible view when he speaks of latitude for future development. Inherent in his words, too, is a recognition that the court is not infallible and that it cannot foresee all future cases. The availability of several judgments gives latitude to later courts. Even if the several judges express substantially the same opinion, the variation in their words is certain to become significant in some subsequent case that perhaps none of them has foreseen.

The truth is that courts do legislate and this is recognized by every judge, though, to use the words that A. P. Herbert put in the mouth of one of his fictitious judges: "The agreeable fiction is that the decision was there already, though hidden till that day in the inexhaustible womb of the common law."[22]

An American judge said:

It always gives an appearance of greater authority to a conclusion to deduce it dialectically from conceded premises than to confess that it involves the appraisal of conflicting interests, which are necessarily incommensurable....[23]

There is reason for the judges to underemphasize their legislative function, for they are not elected, and their appointment is based on their presumed adjudicative skills, not on their wisdom as policy-makers. Another American judge said: "I recognize without hesitation that judges do and must legislate, but they do so only interstitially; they are confined from molar to molecular motions."[24]

---

20 *Saunders v. Anglia Bldg. Society,* [1971] A.C. 1004 at 1015 (H.L.).

21 "The common law is not a brooding omnipresence in the sky but the articulate voice of some sovereign or quasi-sovereign that can be identified", *Southern Pacific Co. v. Jensen,* 244 U. S. 205 at 222 (1917) *per* Holmes J., dissenting.

22 A.P. Herbert, *Uncommon Law,* (1959 ed.), p. 156, *Sparrow v. Pip: The Lords Rebel.*

23 Learned Hand J., dissenting in *Spector Motor Service, Inc. v. Walsh,* 139 F. (2d) 809 at 823 (1944).

24 Holmes J., in *Southern Pacific Co. v. Jensen,* above, note 21 at 221, quoted by Dickson J. in *Harrison v. Carswell;* see above, p. 11.

An approach adopted by some courts in recent years is to look not just at the rule laid down by a previous case but at the reason underlying the rule. If the reason is inapplicable to the circumstances of the present case the rule must be restated. Thus, it was long thought to be a rule that awards of damages in an English court must be in sterling currency. At a time of falling value of the pound, this rule seemed unfair to foreign creditors and it was reversed. When the matter came before the Court of Appeal most observers considered that court bound by the old rule, but Lord Denning M.R. (Master of the Rolls, the title of the Head of the Court of Appeal) said that the rule was originally framed when sterling was stronger than other currencies and, since that fact had changed, the rule should be modified.[25] His conclusion was eventually supported by the House of Lords,[26] though the law lords disapproved of the Court of Appeal taking it on itself to change the law. In another case the question arose of whether a buyer of gasoline could obtain a decree of specific performance (that is, an order specifically requiring supplies to be continued). The judge said:

> Now I come to the most serious hurdle in the way of the plaintiff company which is the well-known doctrine that the court refuses specific performance of a contract to sell and purchase chattels not specific or ascertained. That is a well-established and salutary rule. . . . However, the ratio behind the rule is, as I believe, that under the ordinary contract for the sale of non-specific goods, damages are a sufficient remedy. That, to my mind, is lacking in the circumstances of the present case. . . . Here, the defendant company appears for practical purposes to be the plaintiff company's sole means of keeping its business going, and I am prepared . . . to depart from the general rule. . . .[27]

It is plain that this approach introduces so great a degree of flexibility as to threaten the principle of *stare decisis* itself. If a judge can make her own assessment of the "true reason" for any rule, and then modify the rule in the light of her view of the current merits of the true reason, there is little left of any binding rule of precedent at all.

The common law system, while attaining stability by the application of *stare decisis* manages to maintain at the same time a large measure of flexibility. Lord Mansfield, an eighteenth-century judge, saw this

---

25 *Schorsch Meier G.m.b.H. v. Hennin,* [1975] Q.B. 416 (C.A.).

26 *Miliangos v. George Frank (Textiles) Ltd.,* [1976] A.C. 433 (H.L.). It can never be part of the *ratio decidendi* of a House of Lords decision that the Court of Appeal should have considered itself bound by earlier authority. If the substantive conclusion of the Court of Appeal is correct the House of Lords is bound to affirm it, however much it may disapprove the conduct of the Court of Appeal.

27 *Sky Petroleum Ltd. v. V.I.P. Petroleum Ltd.,* [1974] 1 W.L.R. 576 at 578-9 (Ch. D.) *per* Goulding J.

flexibility as one of the chief merits of the common law as compared with statute. He said:

> All occasions do not arise at once . . . a statute very seldom can take in all cases, therefore the common law *that works itself pure* by rules drawn from the fountain of justice, is for this reason superior to an act of parliament.[28]

Choice of metaphor depends, of course, on attitudes. Slavery is a common source of metaphorical allusions, and many judges have refused "slavishly" to follow prior decisions that they dislike. No one is in favour of slavery. On the other hand, it has been said that it is enslavement to a chart and compass that gives us the freedom of the seas. A modern judge, whom no one could describe as a slavish adherent to precedent, has suggested another metaphor:

> I would treat the [doctrine of precedent] as you would a path through the woods. You must follow it certainly so as to reach your end. But you must not let the path become too overgrown. You must cut out the dead wood and trim off the side branches, else you will find yourself lost in thickets and brambles. My plea is simply to keep the path to justice clear of obstructions which would impede it.[29]

Where no relevant distinction can be discerned, decisions of superior courts are binding on lower courts. The Supreme Court of Canada is not bound by its own previous decisions and several times in recent years has overruled them. In a case decided in 1982, the Court pointed out that, if *stare decisis* led to retention of an unworkable rule it would increase, rather than decrease, uncertainty. Dickson J. said:

> The traditional justification for the *stare decisis* principle is certainty in the law. This of course remains an important consideration even though this Court has announced its willingness, for compelling reasons, to overturn a prior decision. . . . In this instance adherence to the *stare decisis* principle would generate more uncertainty than certainty.[30]

The question of whether an intermediate Court of Appeal is bound by its own decisions is more difficult. The English Court of Appeal considers itself bound, and some Canadian provincial appellate courts have taken the same view. This view depends on the existence of a higher court able to correct errors. As the Supreme Court of Canada becomes more reluctant to hear appeals on points of provincial law the case for permitting the provincial appellate court to overrule its own decisions grows stronger.

---

28 *Per* Lord Mansfield, arguing, as counsel in *Omychund v. Barker* (1744), 1 Atk. 21 at 33.

29 Lord Denning, *The Discipline of Law* (1979), p. 314.

30 *Minister of Indian Affairs and Northern Development v. Ranville*, [1982] 2 S.C.R. 518 at 527-8.

RES JUDICATA AND STARE DECISIS

An English judge once said: "A case is only authority for what it actually decides. I entirely deny that it can ever be quoted for a proposition that may seem to flow logically from it."[31] Taken literally, this view would destroy the doctrine of *stare decisis,* for a case only *actually* decides the issue between the parties to it, and every application of the decision to another case involves an element of abstraction, that is, a judgment that the differences between the first case and the second are not legally material. A judicial decision has two separate effects. It determines an issue between the parties to a dispute, and it establishes some rule or principle for the future. Every decision is at once an application of the law and a contribution to the fabric of the law itself.

All legal systems have a rule that a judicial determination of a case is final. Human institutions are imperfect. Courts will commit errors,[32] but decided cases cannot be reopened simply on an allegation of error. If judicial determination of cases were not final, the legal system would be failing to fulfill its chief purpose, that is, dispute settlement. The rule of finality, often called *res judicata* (matter adjudicated) can at times seem to come into direct conflict with principles of substantive law. Suppose a taxpayer disputes an assessment of income tax, loses, and pays. A month later the Supreme Court of Canada decides a case just like his that establishes that no tax was payable after all. This is very galling to the taxpayer but he has no remedy. His case cannot be heard again (assuming it is too late for an appeal), though had it been delayed for a month it would have been decided differently. Further, if A and B are two taxpayers in identical circumstances, and A's case is heard before the Supreme Court of Canada decision, and B's afterwards, the court will be compelled to decide identical cases in contrary ways.

A case in which the court was faced very starkly with such a conflict between finality and justice was *Re Waring.*[33] A and B were beneficiaries under a single provision in a will. They were left annuities to be paid by the trustees of the will tax-free. A question arose as to whether the effect of a certain statute was to reduce the amount payable under this provision. A litigated the case in 1942,[34] and lost in the Court of Appeal. The trustees then reduced both annuities. In 1946, in another case, the House of Lords held that the Court of Appeal in 1942 had been wrong and that the effect

---

31 Lord Halsbury, above, note 7.

32 Even Jessel M. R., a nineteenth-century judge not lacking in self-confidence, said "I may be wrong, I sometimes am," though he added "but I never doubt." Quoted in Megarry, *Miscellany-at-Law,* p. 8.

33 *Re Waring; Westminster Bank v. Burton-Butler,* [1948] Ch. 221.

34 *Re Waring; Westminster Bank Ltd. v. Awdry,* [1942] Ch. 426 (C.A.).

of the statute was not to reduce the amount payable. A and B then demanded payment of the full amount. It seems a strange result that the court should hold that two beneficiaries in identical circumstances were to be treated differently. What of the principle that like cases are to be decided alike? Yet the anomaly is inescapable. A is bound by the 1942 case and cannot reopen the same issue. B is entitled, according to the law as declared by the House of Lords in 1946, to be paid in full. It was held that A was entitled only to the reduced amount, but that B could claim the full amount, including arrears, that ought to have been paid according to the 1946 decision of the House of Lords.

ENGLISH, AMERICAN AND COMMONWEALTH CASES

The beginning law student is often surprised at the extent to which English cases are still relied on by Canadian courts. Only decisions of higher Canadian courts are actually binding, but Canadian courts continue to treat English decisions with great respect. Canadian common law has maintained a very close association with English law that is only gradually diminishing. American cases, until recently, have less often been cited in Canadian courts, but they are treated as persuasive and are coming to be increasingly relied on especially in areas such as securities regulation where Canadian statutes are based on American models. The adoption of the Charter of Rights and Freedoms in 1982 has led to greater interest in American cases that deal with similar provisions in the U.S. constitution. Commonwealth decisions, particularly Australian ones, are also treated as persuasive.

The question has sometimes arisen of the effect of the overruling in England of a case that has been accepted in Canada. Suppose that the English Court of Appeal decides case A, and the Supreme Court of Canada in case B declares that the rule in case A is part of Canadian law. Then the House of Lords in case C overrules case A. Theoretically, the rule in case A has (by the decision in case B) become part of Canadian law binding on all lower courts. But if the Supreme Court of Canada in case B dealt with the matter very cursorily, whereas the House of Lords in case C gave it careful consideration, it seems unduly rigid to treat case B as absolutely binding. The result would be that the rule in case A, abandoned in the land of its birth and perhaps everywhere else for, let us suppose, very good reason, is still binding on Canadian courts until the Supreme Court of Canada finds the occasion to reverse it. Some follow this view but, in my opinion, a lower court in such circumstances should be free to follow either case A or case C. It is one thing for the Supreme Court of Canada, after careful consideration, to depart from a modern English case. Lower courts would be bound to follow the Supreme Court of Canada.

It is quite another thing, however, for Canadian courts to find themselves bound, against reason, to adhere to an old English decision abandoned as obsolete in England and everywhere else.

LEGAL FICTIONS

The history of English law contains some fantastic fictions. Fictitious claims would be made by plaintiffs with fictitious names against fictitious defendants. Results were often justified on the basis of a palpable fiction, for instance, the result that the defendant should pay the plaintiff a sum of money was often rested on the basis that the defendant had promised to do so, when it was plain that he had made no such promise in fact.[35] A modern critic is apt to be impatient with such fictions: "How can it serve the cause of justice for the judges themselves to be telling lies?"

Professor Lon Fuller of Harvard University has given a modern example of the use of legal fictions that evokes somewhat more sympathy for the practice.[36] The law used to be that trespassers on land could not sue the occupier if they were injured on his land. The case arises of a child attracted onto land by dangerous mining equipment left unfenced and unprotected. When the child is injured it seems at first that the court cannot give her a remedy because she is a trespasser. A way around this result was to hold that the occupier of land had, by leaving attractive machinery in a place accessible to children, impliedly permitted the children to come on his land. The result was that the child was magically transformed from trespasser to implied licensee and recovered her damages. A satisfactory result, most would say, but it rests on an undoubted fiction. The occupier did not permit the child to come on to his land. Why does the judge simply not say what he means? The answer is that if the judge had said: "The law about trespassers is absurd and I will not apply it," the defendant would promptly and successfully have appealed and the child would have ended by losing her award and paying the defendant's costs in two courts. Judges cannot divorce themselves from the framework of legal thought in which they operate. They can legislate but only interstitially. We, as modern critics, should perhaps have the humility to accept the possibility that we too may be enslaved by our own framework of thought, which will seem equally absurd to later generations.

Indeed, it is a legal fiction that enables the common law to retain its flexibility and to develop its doctrines to meet changing social needs. Suppose that there exists a firmly established common law rule that has ceased to meet modern needs. As the rule seems to lead to an unjust result

---

35 The principle is called quasi-contract — as if it were a contract.
36 L. Fuller, *Legal Fictions*, 1967.

in particular cases, the courts will find ways of evading it. Perhaps in the most outrageous cases legislation will reverse the effect of the rule. In other cases lip service to the old rule is maintained, but by a variety of exceptions, explanations and refinements, it will in practice be as often avoided as applied. Finally the rule is so undermined by exceptions that it has become an empty shell, and a court can renounce it, or restate it so as to accord with actual practice without itself making any significant change in the law. No court in this process of development takes it on itself to usurp the role of the legislature by reversing the old rule. The courts that make exceptions continue lip service to the rule; the court that finally renounces the rule does it simply as a recognition of the actual current state of the law.

LAW REPORTS AND DIGESTS

An essential part of the common law system is reliable reporting of decided cases. In former times judges were often critical of the reliability of reports, one judge going so far as to say: "[S]ee the inconveniences of these scambling reports, they will make us appear to posterity for a parcel of blockheads."[37] Errors creep into even modern reports, but the editors and publishers of them have been spared judicial rebukes of this severity.

In Canada there are many series of reports, some general, some covering specific courts, others dealing with specific subject-matters. Not all decided cases are reported. The editors of law reports select those that seem to them most important and interesting. The most general series is the Dominion Law Reports (D.L.R.) which publishes about ten volumes a year covering matters of general legal interest from all courts in Canada. An annotation service enables the user to trace later references to reported cases. A list of the major Canadian reports is given in Appendix C.

In citing cases, the date is given in round brackets if the volumes of the series cited are numbered sequentially. But if the date is itself part of the volume reference it is given in square brackets. Compare the following two citations of the same case:

J.S. Ellis and Co. v. Willis (1972), 30 D.L.R. (3d) 397 (Ont. H. C.)
J.S. Ellis and Co. v. Willis, [1973] 1 O.R. 121 (H.C.)

In the first citation the reference is complete without the date; the reader could find Volume 30 of the third series of the Dominion Law Reports and the date is added for information. The date is the actual date of the judgment. In the second citation the date is in effect part of the

---

37   Holt C.J., in *Slater v. May* (1704), 2 Ld. Raym. 1071 at 1072.

volume number. It is given in square brackets and is not necessarily the actual date of the judgment, the latter being added (in round brackets) only where it differs materially from the volume date. It is usual in either case to add the name of the court in round brackets at the end of the citation, unless this is obvious from the rest of the citation or from the context. In American case citations, the date (always in round brackets) is usually given at the end of the citation, with the name of the court.

Digests are volumes containing summaries of decided cases organized by subject-matter. They vary in the amount of synthesis and commentary they provide. The Canadian Encyclopedic Digest, for example, is a general treatise on Canadian case law with cases cited as footnotes to a continuous text. On the other hand, the Canadian Abridgment is a collection of case summaries with no commentary. In recent years a number of loose-leaf services have been introduced in particular specialized areas such as Income Tax. These are heavily relied on by practising lawyers in keeping up-to-date both with statutory change and with common law developments. Appendix C lists the most important Canadian digests and loose-leaf services.

8

EQUITY

THE COURT OF CHANCERY

Until about a hundred years ago there were two separate legal systems existing side by side. These were known as common law and equity.

The Court of Equity, commonly called Chancery, was originally set up to alleviate the rigidity of the common law. A litigant dissatisfied with a result obtainable from a court of law could appeal to the Chancellor, an official who acted as the king's deputy, for relief. Equity originated as an entirely discretionary power (originally in the sovereign, later delegated to the Chancellor) to grant relief on grounds of natural justice and fairness. In the course of time, however, rules grew up to govern the Chancellor's discretion, and by the nineteenth century the system of equity had become even more rigid than the common law that it was supposed to ameliorate. The ill reputation of the court even became part of the language. Dictionaries give "in Chancery" as meaning in an awkward predicament or (in boxing) having one's head under one's opponent's arm. Readers of Dickens will recall his vivid description of the Court of Chancery in *Bleak House:*

> Fog everywhere . . . and hard by Temple Bar in Lincoln's Inn Hall at the very heart of the fog, sits the Lord High Chancellor in his High Court of Chancery. . . . This is the Court of Chancery; which has its decaying houses and its blighted lands in every shire; which has its worn out lunatic in every madhouse, and its dead in every churchyard; which has its ruined suitor, with his slipshod heels and threadbare dress, borrowing and begging through the round of every man's acquaintance; which gives to monied might the means abundantly of wearying out the right; which so exhausts finances, patience, courage, hope; so overthrows the brain and breaks the heart; that there is not an honourable man among its practitioners who would not give — who

does not often give — this warning: "Suffer any wrong that can be done you, rather than come here!"[1]

Every legal system must contain elements of certainty, predictability and stability on the one hand, and elements of flexibility, fairness and justice in the individual case on the other. It is a peculiarity of our legal system that these two competing sets of values were in a sense institutionalized in the two separate systems of law and equity. It is an interesting reflection that the system of equity proved unable to maintain its flexibility. The search for order and stability led to rules, principles and guidelines to canalize the Chancellor's "discretion" and to make it certain and predictable. It was said disparagingly of the early court that justice varied according to the length of the Chancellor's foot. Recently a judge remarked that in the nineteenth century the Chancellor's foot was replaced by the Vice-Chancellor's footrule (that is, too broad a discretion was replaced by too rigid an application of mechanical rules).[2]

Until the late nineteenth century the courts of law and equity were completely separate. Since equity represented an attempt to rectify deficiencies in the law there were many instances of direct conflict between legal and equitable rules. Commonly a person with legal title to land would be prevented by the Court of Equity from exercising those legal rights. In such cases of conflict, the equitable rule prevailed, because the Chancellor enforced his orders by threat of imprisonment for contempt. The Court of Chancery would, if necessary, even order a person not to enforce legal rights or not to institute or continue an action at law (such an order of the Court of Chancery was called a common injunction). This extraordinary relationship of the two systems led one commentator to say that England had one court set up to administer injustice and another to stop it.[3]

The Judicature Act (1875 in England, 1881 in Ontario, slightly different dates in other provinces) brought about a fusion of the two courts. Now a single court administers both law and equity. Consequently the interaction and net result of a legal right subject to an equitable defence can now be determined by a single court. The effect is that in the modern court equity prevails, just as it did before the Judicature Act.

THE MODERN COURT

However, the fusion of the courts did not in itself cause a fusion of law and equity, and it is still necessary in some cases to determine whether

---

1 Dickens, *Bleak House,* Everyman ed., pp. 1-3.
2 Lord Simon in *Steadman v. Steadman,* [1976] A. C. 536 at 560. See above, p. 53.
3 Cited in Williams, *Learning the Law,* 8th ed., p. 27.

a right would, before 1881, have been legal or equitable. Here is an example. An innocent misrepresentation inducing the making of a contract gave to the party deceived an equitable right to avoid the contract, but no right to damages because the Court of Equity did not award damages. This restriction has been carried forward, and modern courts have asserted that there is still no power to award damages for innocent misrepresentation. This may at first seem strange for the modern court plainly does have power, as heir to the old common law court, to award damages. But the reasoning is that the modern court can do anything that a court of law could have done before 1881 and everything that a Court of Equity could have done before 1881 but that the Judicature Act does not require it to assert a power that neither court formerly had, that is, to award a legal remedy for an equitable "wrong". Another instance concerns defences. The Court of Equity recognized a number of defences to equitable rights that were not recognized as defences to legal rights in a court of law. So it still happens in the modern court that a plaintiff attempting to assert an equitable right may be defeated on the ground that she has been guilty of, say, sharp practice, or unfair delay, whereas her legal rights would not be affected by the same defences.

Though one can appreciate the historical basis for these distinctions, it still seems anomalous that a modern court feels compelled to restrict its own powers by reference to those of courts abolished over a hundred years ago. A more satisfactory approach would, it is suggested, be for the modern court to recognize that though it is not *required* by the Judicature Act to assume a power to award damages for innocent misrepresentation, it has the power inherited from both the old courts to develop remedies that are apt for the modern administration of justice. Again, if a plaintiff is guilty of sharp practice or of delay that seems unfair, the modern court should ask what consequences ought to flow from the misconduct in question. If the consequence should be that some sorts of remedy, but not others, should be abridged or restricted, let the court give effect to that consequence without regard to whether the rights abridged were, before 1881, legal or equitable rights. It should be no obstacle that some development of the law is needed from what it was in 1881.

EQUITABLE DOCTRINES

The most important concept of equity is the trust, and the origins of the trust illustrate the way in which equitable rules developed. A conveys his land to B, not intending it really to become B's, but for some special purpose, in mediaeval times often to avoid the feudal obligations of land tenure. At law the land was B's (having been duly conveyed) but if B, in breach of the understanding on which the land was conveyed, attempted to keep it for himself to the exclusion of A, the Chancellor would intervene to prevent the inequity to A. The Chancellor could not directly override B's title — he was, after all, the lawful owner. But he could achieve substantially the same result by declaring that B held the land "to the use" of A, or on "trust" for A. B was then held to be a trustee, and subject to onerous duties to hold and use the land entirely for A's benefit. Thus, B's paper title was made completely useless to him without any direct confrontation with the law.

Another example is the case of a will made in favour of B. After the testator's death A proves that the testator intended the property really to be A's, that B was simply to look after it until A should come of age, and that B had agreed to this arrangement. The Wills Act clearly provides that property can only be given away on death according to the terms of a document signed in the presence of two witnesses.[4] Indeed, the whole purpose of the Wills Act is to avoid disputes of the sort raised by A in this case. Equally plainly, it would be offensive to most people's sense of justice to allow B to keep what most people would say is A's money. We might even be inclined to stigmatize B's conduct as "fraudulent". The Court of Equity thought the same and made B a trustee for the benefit of A, thereby completely reversing the effect of the Wills Act.

Even in the modern court the concept of the trust continues to enable the courts to circumvent statutory rules. For example, the law clearly states that on the death of a person without a will his next-of-kin inherit his property. In a modern Nova Scotia case, a woman and a man lived together for many years in the mistaken belief that they were married to each other, fully expecting that the woman would inherit the man's property on his death. He died without a will. A statute clearly provided that his relatives were to take the property, but the court plainly felt it unjust that the woman who had lived with him for so long should be disinherited. MacKeigan C.J.N.S., found the solution as follows:

> I believe that the solution of the problem rests in the law of trusts, that versatile handmaiden of equity, without using any fictions, stretching any facts or distorting any principles of law or equity. The heirs at law on Mr. Spears' death received legal title to his lands and goods, but did so subject to the equitable rights of Mrs. Spears [that is, the woman who had lived with the deceased]. Those rights gave rise to a constructive trust requiring the heirs to deliver his lands and goods up to her. The constructive trust is invoked to prevent unjust enrichment of the heirs, to ensure they do not get what they have no right to get. As Judge Cardozo said:

---

4 In some provinces, a will written entirely in the testator's handwriting (a holograph will) is also valid.

" . . . A constructive trust is the formula through which the conscience of equity finds expression. When property has been acquired in such circumstances that the holder of the legal title may not in good conscience retain the beneficial interest, equity converts him into a trustee."[5]

The plain truth is that the court has overridden the provisions of the statute because it considers them unfair.

The trust, originally invented to avoid injustice, came to be seen as a useful device for dividing ownership, and the deliberate establishment of trusts enables modern lawyers to design flexible dispositions of property often in order to minimize the incidence of various taxes on income and property.

Equity has also played an important part in developing remedies, especially for breach of contract. The common law courts would give only an award of damages, but often an aggrieved plaintiff wants a specific remedy, such as an order directing the defendant to do just what she promised to do, or refrain from doing what she has promised not to do. The Courts of Equity would grant such remedies. So, where a vendor of land refused to convey, the purchaser could only get a money award at law, but in equity he could get what is called an order of specific performance, compelling conveyance of the particular land. Again, if A sells her business to B and promises not to compete, but then opens up shop next door, B will rarely be satisfied with a money award; the amount of his loss is hard to prove, and in any case he would not thereby receive what was promised to him. In equity, he can obtain an injunction (enforceable by threat of imprisonment) compelling A to close her shop. There are a number of other remedies developed by equity that have a very significant effect on substantive rights. For example, written contractual documents were said to be conclusive of the parties' legal rights, but if convinced that the document misstated the parties' true agreement, the Court of Equity would "reform" or "rectify" the document — that is, put it right. This simple notion substantially abridged the effect of the legal rule of conclusiveness of documents. Again, it was said to be irrelevant at law that an agreement was harsh or unfair, but the Courts of Equity would "rescind", that is, annul, an agreement for what was called unconscionability — a degree of unfairness that affected the Chancellor's conscience. Plainly, again, the legal rule that contracts are binding is now subject to an exception which, according to the tenderness of the Chancellor's conscience, might swallow up the whole rule. Again, an innocent misrepresentation inducing a contract was irrelevant at law, but equity would grant rescission for misrepresentation on the very simple ground that it was unfair for a person to profit by a statement that he

5 *Re Spears and Levy* (1974), 52 D.L.R. (3d) 146 at 154 (N.S.C.A.).

now (at the time of litigation) knows to be false. It will be appreciated from these examples that a legal rule taken alone can be very misleading — the equitable gloss may utterly reverse its effect. Despite the rigidity that had infected the system of equity by the nineteenth century one can still see the operation, even in the modern law, of the simple principles of fairness and good conscience cutting through the complexities of legal rules.

The ancient role of equity, as representing the element of flexibility in the legal system, is once again beginning to assert itself. Some modern judges, notably Lord Denning of the English Court of Appeal, have been fully conscious that they are heirs of the old Chancellors as well as of the common law judges. Law and equity have been described as two streams flowing side by side in a common channel: "the two streams of jurisdiction, though they run in the same channel, run side by side and do not mingle their waters."[6] In 1977 an English judge said that this metaphor had become "mischievous and deceptive." He added:

> As at the confluence of the Rhône and Saône, it may be possible for a short distance to discern the source from which each part of the combined stream came, but there comes a point at which this ceases to be possible. If Professor Ashburner's fluvial metaphor is to be retained at all, the waters of the confluent streams of laws and equity have surely mingled now.[7]

---

6 Ashburner, *Principles of Equity* (1902), p. 23.
7 *United Scientific Holdings, Ltd. v. Burnley Borough Council,* [1978] A.C. 904 at 925 (H.L.) *per* Lord Diplock.

9

STATUTES

LEGISLATIVE SUPREMACY

The Constitution Act of 1867 (formerly called the British North America Act) declares in its preamble that Canada is to have a constitution similar in principle to that of the United Kingdom. This was taken as an affirmation of the principle of legislative supremacy. Though an early English court once suggested that Parliament itself could not validly legislate contrary to the law of God, and in 1614 a court said: "Even an Act of Parliament made against natural equity, as to make a man judge in his own case, is void in itself,"[1] it has long been the settled view in England that Parliament is absolutely supreme and can enact any law it wishes. The courts are interpreters only, and cannot override the parliamentary will.

In the United States, on the other hand, the idea of the supremacy of the law of God or (in its secular form) natural law, took strong hold. Though the original constitution contained no restrictions on legislation, the first ten amendments, proposed by Congress in 1789 and ratified in 1791, constitute what became known as the Bill of Rights. These amendments, together with some later additions, declare fundamental freedoms, and the United States courts have interpreted them to restrict the powers of Congress and of the State legislatures. The values affirmed by the Bill of Rights are necessarily in very general terms. "Congress shall make no law . . . abridging the freedom of speech."[2] Taken literally this would abolish laws governing official secrets, sedition, incitement to mutiny or other crime, and defamation. Of course, it cannot and has not been construed so widely. Some reasonable and necessary restrictions on

---

1 *Day v. Savadge* (1614), Hob. 85 at 87.
2 First Amendment.

freedom of speech must be preserved. But only the Supreme Court of the United States can say what restrictions are reasonable and necessary, and so ultimately it is the Supreme Court that makes the law on freedom of speech, as on many other key social questions in the United States, such as the civil rights of minority groups and the limits of police powers (equal protection of the laws and due process of law).

The Canadian position is something of a compromise between the English and American views. In 1982, a significant step was taken towards the American view by the adoption, in the Canadian constitution, of a Charter of Rights and Freedoms. There is a general provision that the Charter is subject to "such reasonable limits prescribed by law as can be demonstrably justified in a free and democratic society." This may have been intended by the drafters as some concession to the principle of legislative supremacy, but its effect has been to require the courts to make the necessary balances.

A more significant concession is the provision that Parliament or the legislature of a province may expressly override the Charter by declaring that an Act shall operate notwithstanding a provision of the Charter on fundamental freedoms, or legal or equality rights.

The Charter has been very often invoked in the first ten years of its operation, and has been used more frequently than most of its supporters in 1982 expected. The effect has been to bring many matters that were formerly considered purely political into the judicial sphere. There have been only a few uses of the "override" provision by provincial legislatures.

The principle of legislative supremacy is also modified by the federal character of the Canadian State. The Constitution Act of 1867 (formerly called the British North America Act), the central constitutional document of Canada, was in form an Act of the United Kingdom Parliament, though in substance the product of agreement among the representatives of the four original Canadian provinces. The Act divides legislative power by subject-matter between the Parliament of Canada and the legislatures of the provinces. Thus, although complete legislative power (subject now to the Charter of Rights) is given to Parliament and the legislatures together, each acting alone has only restricted powers. In case of dispute it is for the court to say whether or not Parliament, or a legislature, has exceeded its powers. The decisions of the courts, first the Judicial Committee of the Privy Council (which was the highest Canadian court until 1949)[3] and more recently the Supreme Court of Canada, have played a very important role in moulding the present shape of Confederation. It is ironic that much of the language of the Constitution Act leans more towards central powers than the corresponding language of the United States'

---

3 Criminal appeals were abolished in 1933; civil appeals continued until 1949.

constitution, and yet, largely because of the judicial interpretation, the federal Congress in the United States has much wider powers in practice than the Parliament of Canada. An example is offered by the trade and commerce power. The United States' constitution gives Congress power "to regulate commerce . . . among the several states."[4] The corresponding Canadian phrase gives the Parliament of Canada power to legislate in respect of "trade and commerce."[5] Anyone would think that the Canadian phrase gives the wider power. It includes both trade and commerce and is not restricted to "interprovincial" trade and commerce. Yet the American phrase has been interpreted to give Congress virtually unlimited powers, whereas in Canada the trade and commerce power has been very restrictively construed.

The original British North America Act contained no amending formula, and, until 1982, the only method of amendment (with limited exceptions) was for the United Kingdom Parliament, on the request of the Canadian Parliament, to enact the desired amendment. This procedure was undoubtedly anomalous, but continued so long as it did because of the failure of the provinces to agree on an amending formula. In 1982 a formula was eventually agreed on by every province except Quebec and enacted by the United Kingdom Parliament, but it contains an anomaly of its own, for it provides (in respect of certain important amendments) that an amendment shall not have effect in any province that dissents from it. It remains to be seen how this "opting out" procedure will work in practice. But it is clear that the role of the United Kingdom Parliament in Canadian constitutional affairs is now at an end.

THE PROCESS OF LEGISLATION

A bill becomes law when it has been enacted by the legislature (in the case of federal bills by both Houses of Parliament) and has received royal assent. A bill goes through three stages. "First reading" is a formal introduction of the bill, which is printed and made available for public comment. Many bills, even government bills, never pass this stage, but are replaced or withdrawn in the light of public reaction. "Second reading" is approval in principle of the bill, which is then referred in appropriate cases to a committee for detailed study. "Third reading" is final approval. Royal assent is now a formality and is always forthcoming on enactment of a bill. Frequently, however, a bill will contain a provision that it is to come into force on a day to be fixed by proclamation. The consequence of such a provision is that the bill is law, but does not come into effect

---

4 Article 1, s. 8.
5 Constitution Act, 1867 (U.K.), s. 91.2.

until the government chooses. This enables the government to delay bringing a statute into effect so as to enable those affected by it to learn of its provisions and to make appropriate adjustments in their affairs. Sometimes, too, the delay is used to make last-minute amendments.

All federal and provincial statutes are published in annual volumes. The provisions of an Act that has been amended several times may, therefore, be spread over a number of volumes. At intervals of approximately ten to fifteen years a set of consolidated statutes is issued, called revised statutes. These serve the purpose of consolidating amendments, and reprinting most (but not necessarily all) of the general statutes in force. Statutes are cited by reference to the chapter number in the latest revision, for example, R.S.O. 1990, c. D.5 (Revised Statutes of Ontario, Chapter D.5). Enactments subsequent to the latest revision are cited: Stat. Ont. (or S.O.) 1981, c. 26. Alternatively statutes may be cited by the name of the statute followed by the province in round brackets and the chapter number: 1981 (Ont.), c. 26. The older method of citing statutes was by the regnal year: 20 Eliz. II, c. 26, but this method is now falling out of favour, partly because of the inconvenient arithmetic required, and partly because the citation fails to distinguish between Ontario statutes and those of other Commonwealth jurisdictions. Modern statutes have a short title included in the text of the statute itself, for example, The Family Law Act, 1986. The revised statutes include indexes, but these are quite inadequate and wholly unreliable as research tools.

REGULATIONS

Much law-making is effected by subordinate legislation known as regulations. The statute itself empowers the government (formally the Governor-General or the Lieutenant-Governor, or in some cases, a Minister, board, commission or tribunal) to make law without further legislation. By this means detailed provisions need not be debated in the legislature, and flexibility can be maintained to enable the government to act quickly to meet an unexpected case without initiating new legislation. The attractions of this approach to a government are readily apparent. Suppose a government proposes a law to establish minimum wages, but it is generally agreed that payment of minimum wages will impose too great a burden on certain classes of employers. A debate in the legislature on the precise classes of employers to be exempted will be time-consuming, divisive, and will certainly leave gaps and anomalies. It is much easier to enact that all employers shall pay minimum wages, but that the Lieutenant-Governor may make regulations exempting certain classes of employers from the operation of the Act. Then the regulations can be quickly and easily enacted, amended and repealed as experience suggests. The regulations when passed have the force of the statute itself.

With the advantages of wide powers of subordinate legislation come certain drawbacks. The power of exempting from minimum wage regulations, for example, has the effect of withdrawing from debate a key aspect of the legislation. This enables a government to withdraw difficult issues from public scrutiny. It is too easy to avoid a difficult issue by drafting universal rules and then making exceptions later by regulation. In a sense, the legislature gives up its law-making responsibility to the government which is given power to make the legislation fully effective or wholly ineffective at its discretion. Every power to make regulations amounts to a suspension of Parliamentary democracy, an extreme example being the former War Measures Act,[6] which empowered the government to make by Order in Council (that is, by government order without prior Parliamentary approval) any laws it deemed advisable for the security, defence, peace, order and welfare of Canada. There is a danger, too, that a government given wide law-making powers will be susceptible to behind-the-scenes influences of powerful interest groups. Perhaps, for example, the agricultural industry will find it easier than it should to persuade a government dependent on rural votes that payment of minimum wages to farm workers would be ruinous to farmers. Although legislative committees exist with power to refer regulations to the legislature, the power is not often exercised. It is an increasingly common practice for governments to consult with interested parties before promulgating regulations.

Even more important than government regulations are regulations and decisions made by administrative tribunals. Thousands of regulatory tribunals and individuals exercising statutory powers affect every aspect of our lives in the modern State. As a practical matter regulatory tribunals are as important a source of law, both regulatory and adjudicative, as the legislatures and the courts themselves.

Regulations are published in the Canada Gazette and in the provincial Gazettes. Federal regulations, and some provincial regulations, are consolidated periodically like the statutes. So, for example, there is a volume of revised regulations of Ontario for 1980. Subsequent annual volumes with cumulative indexes enable a searcher to discover what regulations have been passed under a particular statute. Regulations are cited, like statutes, by reference to the latest revision (R.R.O. 1980, Reg. 94). Subsequent regulations are cited Ont. Reg. (or 0. Reg.) 836/81 (that is, Regulation 836 of 1981).

---

6 R.S.C. 1970, c. W-2, repealed R.S.C. 1985, c. 22 (4th Supp.), s. 80.

PROCESS OF INTERPRETATION

It might be supposed that the uncertainty inherent in judicial development of legal rules will be absent in the case of statutory enactment. If a statute governs a question there can surely be no room for argument; we need only look at the terms of the Act.

Statutory interpretation is not, however, a mechanical process. Consider, for example, a case in which the Ontario Divisional Court had to determine whether or not a mushroom was a vegetable (they held by a majority of two to one that it was).[7] The first reaction of a person on hearing that the Divisional Court has decided that a mushroom is a vegetable might be to say "How absurd; don't the judges have any serious issues to occupy their time?" A moment's reflection will reveal that issues must have been involved that were important enough to someone to be worth arguing in the Divisional Court. A brief look at the case reveals that the question in issue was the interpretation of a regulation under the Employment Standards Act excluding, from certain provisions of the Act, "a person employed on a farm whose employment is directly related to the primary production of eggs, milk, grain, seeds, fruit, vegetables, maple products, honey, tobacco, pigs, cattle, sheep and poultry." A closer look reveals that the "certain provisions" were the minimum wage laws, and the question was whether mushroom farmworkers had to be paid minimum wages. So far from being a trivial question it is one of huge importance to the lives of hundreds, perhaps thousands, of people, that is, the workers and employers in the mushroom business, not to mention mushroom consumers.

The next level of reaction is to say that the judges should leave it to the experts to say whether or not a mushroom is a vegetable. Judges are not mycologists. Let the judge stick to judging and not trespass on the expert fields of other professions. How can a judge make a mushroom into a vegetable? Next they will be telling us that walnuts are cereals. This is, in effect, the view of the dissenting judge.[8] However, the court's decision is a social one that will intimately affect people's lives, and the court cannot close its eyes to the true nature of the decision by retreating into technicalities. The court's duty is not to pronounce on the botanical nature of fungi, but to say whether mushrooms are vegetables *for the purposes of this regulation.* The court cannot escape from deciding whether or not minimum wages are to be paid to mushroom workers.

A third level of reaction to the case is to expect the court to decide the true meaning of "vegetable" within the context of the regulation. Let

---

7 *Ont. Mushroom Co. v. Learie* (1977), 15 O.R. (2d) 639 (Div. Ct.).
8 Southey J.

us look at the social purpose of the exclusion; plainly the legislature intended to exclude farm workers in general, and presumably they meant to treat mushroom growers in the same way as other workers. There is no sensible reason for a distinction, and so the regulation should be interpreted so as to give effect to what the legislature must presumably have intended. This is, by and large, the view taken by the majority in the case.[9] The dissenting judge thus appears as an unimaginative literalist out of touch with reality and unconcerned with the true policy of the regulations.

Perceptions of desirable social objectives can vary, however, and one could imagine a fourth level of reaction to the case. Suppose that farm workers generally and mushroom workers in particular are underpaid and exploited and all right-minded people are boycotting Ontario mushrooms and agitating for better pay for the workers. The majority decision now becomes an unimaginative and predictable maintaining of the status quo, and the dissenting judge, so far from seeming out of touch with reality, becomes the champion of the under-privileged. His reliance on mycologists and dictionaries suddenly ceases to be dull and pedestrian and becomes instead a brilliant technique of achieving justice for the workers.

RULES OF INTERPRETATION

It will be seen from this example that statutory interpretation is an art that can be practised at many levels. Various rules and principles have evolved, but they do not assist in the difficult cases. Consider the three so-called rules of statutory interpretation, the literal rule, the golden rule and the mischief rule.

The literal rule is that the words in their literal meaning are controlling. It would support the dissenting judge's view of the mushroom case. There is a respectable argument to be made that judges should steer entirely clear of trying to determine the desirability of particular social policies and should simply apply what the legislature says.

The golden rule is that the court must reach a conclusion that avoids absurdities. This tends to support the majority (it would be "absurd" to suppose that the legislature meant to single out mushroom growers for better treatment than all other agricultural workers), though it is not conclusive, since there is nothing inherently "absurd" in paying minimum wages to mushroom workers. Absurdity is often in the eye of the beholder.

The third rule, the mischief rule, requires the court to see what evil or deficiency the statute sought to set right, and to interpret it accordingly. This rule, too, tends to support the majority in the mushroom case (the

---

9 Reid and Maloney JJ.

general purpose of the exception is to exclude agricultural workers from minimum wage laws) but it is not conclusive either, since it would be possible to look at the minimum wage regulations as a whole, and say the mischief aimed at is the payment of wages less than the minimum, and so the regulations are to be so construed as to entitle as many workers as possible to minimum wages.

None of these so-called rules is really a legal rule at all. They represent diverse and self-contradictory approaches. All legal reasoning is result-orientated, as is illustrated by the famous story of the American judge who said: "Judgment for the plaintiff; Mr. Justice Story will furnish the authorities."[10] If the court wants mushroom workers to be paid minimum wages it finds the words of the statute to be plain and unambiguous and it applies the literal rule. If it wants to exclude the payment of minimum wages it will find that such payment would lead to an absurdity and that it is contrary to the general intention of the statute.

Another illustration of the purposive nature of statutory interpretation is the case of the bullet in the suspect's shoulder, mentioned earlier.[11] The court had to interpret section 487 of the Criminal Code empowering the issue of a search warrant to search a building, receptacle or place. Literally the suspect's shoulder blade is a "place", but the literal rule cannot answer the question of the meaning of section 487. Words take their meanings from the context in which they are used. The court cannot escape from the responsibility of deciding whether or not the police ought to be able to extract the bullet. Other principles of statutory interpretation can be brought into play in the bullet case. There is the *ejusdem generis* rule. *Ejusdem generis* means of the same class, and suggests that "place" is to be interpreted to mean "place that is not quite a building or receptacle but is something like a building or receptacle." There is the principle called *noscitur a sociis* (it is known by its associates), that is, "place" is to be interpreted in the light of words used with it, just as in the mushroom case "vegetable" is to be interpreted in the light of the other farm products listed.

A closely related rule of statutory interpretation that shares the distinction of expression in a dead language is *expressio unius exclusio alterius,* that is, the expression of one thing implies the exclusion of the other. If a statute says motor vehicles shall be licensed, one does not require the help of a Latin phrase to conclude that the provision does not apply to bicycles. But suppose the statute says "Licences are required for all vehicles including automobiles, trucks, buses and motorcycles." The question arises whether a bicycle requires a licence. "Vehicle" might, taken

---

10 Cited in Llewellyn, *The Bramble Bush* (1960 ed.), p. 36.

11 Above, pp. 2-3, 52-53.

alone, include a bicycle, but the inclusion of specified classes of vehicles other than bicycles tends to suggest that bicycles are excluded. Statutory drafters often attempt to displace the effect of this rule of interpretation by saying "vehicles, without limiting the generality of the word, shall include . . ." The court is then asked not to use the specified classes to restrict the generality of the word "vehicle". They still have to interpret the true meaning of the word, however, and, as the foregoing discussion shows, words do not have fixed and unalterable meanings. The court will still be in the position of having to determine whether or not bicycles are to have licences. As the mushroom case shows, this is a problem that Latin tags cannot ultimately solve.

The meaning of words often proves elusive in other contexts than statutory interpretation, and the interpretation of wills is a fertile source of litigation. It has often been said that the home-made will is a kind of charitable donation to the legal profession.[12] There is a case of a man who made a will consisting only of three words: "All to mother". Clear enough, one might think, but it was proved that he had always referred to his wife as "Mother" and that his intention had been to benefit her, not his mother.[13]

In some cases words acquire meanings that are on their face absurd. As one judge said, a contract to deliver eau de cologne is hardly to be performed by supplying water from the Rhine river.[14] One who orders a hot dog, or a bottomless cup of coffee, would similarly be disappointed or at least surprised by literal performance.[15] The lawyer in every field must express his meaning by words, but words never have had nor can have fixed and certain meanings. In statutes, wills, contracts and other documents, words can only take meaning from their context.

LEGISLATIVE INTENTION

Courts speak very often in construing statutes of finding the intention of the legislature. The attribution of the result reached to the legislature has the effect of understating the extent to which the court itself is making law. In announcing a common law rule the court often uses language implying that the law is unchanging and that the rule announced is not

---

12 In *Re Gare*, [1952] Ch. 80 [1951] W.N. 564 Harman J. is reported to have said of a testator who had made a will by filling in blanks on a printed form, "The testator signed the will and no doubt thought he had done a good day's work, as for the legal profession, he had." The report in [1952] Ch. in the semi-official law reports series that is revised by the judges before publication, omits this passage.

13 *Thorn v. Dickens*, [1906] W.N. 54.

14 Darling J., in *Lemy v. Watson*, [1915] 3 K.B. 731 at 752.

15 The example is from Megarry, *Miscellany-at-Law*, p. 37.

a new invention of the courts but, at the most, a discovery of a rule that has always existed, or that can be deduced by rational processes from longstanding principles. As the discussion in other chapters of common law reasoning tends to show, there is a good deal more flexibility in the judicial process than is implied by the theory of an unchanging common law, like a "brooding omnipresence in the sky," as Holmes wrote.[16] This theory of the judicial role is more than a gratuitous fiction. It tends to support the constitutional role of the judges as adjudicators rather than as legislators. The judges are not elected, or appointed to be legislators; they are not responsible to the electorate; their view of desirable social policy is entitled to no more respect than any other person's. They can earn and keep public respect as learned adjudicators applying principles that they do not make themselves. They will quickly forfeit that respect if they seem to be setting themselves up as lawmakers, especially in areas of acute social controversy.

So also in the interpretation of statutes the judges are anxious, and for good constitutional reasons, to appear as interpreters and not as manufacturers of law. As one judge said, they can iron out the creases, but they must not alter the material.[17] Hence, the judges emphasize the intention of the legislature, and cast themselves in the role of humble functionaries whose duty it is simply to interpret and apply the will of the all-powerful legislature.

The legislative "intention", however, is, in point of fact, not ascertainable by any means except through the perception of the judge himself. There is no possibility, in interpreting a doubtful statute, of a reference to the legislature, or any representative of it, to ask for clarification. The legislature speaks only through the statute itself, and in case of doubt the judge must do the best he can with the words used.

What about the debates, or governmental announcements discussing and explaining the intention of the statute before its enactment? It might be thought that these would be relevant to an inquiry into legislative intention. However, there are difficulties. Generally, on a difficult point, the explanations will conflict. Take the mushroom case discussed above. An examination of the legislative debate might reveal that the Minister of Labour had said that the purpose of the minimum wage rules was to secure a decent wage for all Ontario workers. An opposition member from a rural area had asked how the rules would affect small farmers who could not afford to pay minimum wages, and the Minister of Agriculture replied that agricultural workers would be exempted by regulation. None of this

---

16 See above, note 21, p. 82.
17 Denning L.J., in *Seaford Court Estates Ltd. v. Asher*, [1949] 2 K.B. 481 at 499; affirmed [1950] A.C. 508 (H.L.).

is much help to the court, which must still determine the meaning of the words actually used (in that case in the regulation, not in the statute itself).

Even where the government controls a majority of the legislature, the expressed intention of the government may not be conclusive. Suppose the Minister of Justice had been specifically asked in Parliament whether the search warrant provisions of the Criminal Code were wide enough to enable the police to extract bullets from suspects' bodies. Suppose again that the Minister of Justice said unequivocally that "place" would include parts of a suspect's body. Should this be conclusive as to the legislative intention? Surely it cannot be. Parliament votes for the words of a bill, not for what the Minister of Justice says they mean. Many members on both sides of the House might have said to themselves: "I hear what the Minister says, but I do not agree with his reading of the bill." The court cannot conclude that every member who voted for the bill voted for the Minister's interpretation of the particular clause in question. Another way of putting the point is that Parliament speaks only through legislation duly enacted: what the Minister says is not an Act of Parliament.

The so-called "mischief" rule mentioned above in practice allows in a good deal of background material to explain the prior deficiencies in the law that the Act aimed to remedy. The House of Lords has affirmed the traditional English rule that parliamentary debates are never admissible. In the United States, on the other hand, legislative debates are readily admitted. The position in Canada is unclear. Recent cases indicate that the court will consider all material that might be relevant to understanding the context of the statute, but will recognize that none of it can be conclusive on the meaning of the words actually used.

10

THE STRUCTURE OF THE COURTS

SUPERIOR PROVINCIAL COURTS

The key to the Canadian court system is the superior court of general jurisdiction in each province. The name of this court varies from province to province. In Ontario it is called the Ontario Court (General Division). In Manitoba, Saskatchewan, Alberta and New Brunswick it is the Court of Queen's Bench. In the other common law provinces it is the Supreme Court, Trial Division (the other division being the appellate division). In Quebec it is the Cour Supérieur. This court is *the* court of justice in each province, not in the sense that it hears more cases or affects more people other than courts. It does not. It is *the* court in the sense that it is the general court with unlimited jurisdiction and unlimited powers to administer the law except insofar as a statute specifically gives exclusive jurisdiction over some particular subject-matter to another tribunal. It is this court that is the successor to the eighteenth-century courts of common law and equity. All other courts, above and below, have been added later.

Over the superior court of original jurisdiction in each province is an appellate court, called the Court of Appeal in British Columbia, Ontario, Manitoba, Saskatchewan, Alberta, New Brunswick and Quebec, and the Appeal or Appellate Division of the Supreme Court in the other provinces. In Ontario there is also a court called the Divisional Court which sits in panels of three judges of the General Division to review decisions, mainly of administrative tribunals. The judges of all these provincial courts are appointed by the government of Canada.

SUPREME COURT OF CANADA

Above the provincial Courts of Appeal sits the Supreme Court of Canada, which hears appeals from the Courts of Appeal from each common law province and from Quebec. The Supreme Court of Canada thus administers both common law and civil law, just as the highest English tribunal, the Appellate Committee of the House of Lords, administers both English and Scottish law. The Supreme Court of Canada also hears appeals from the Federal Court of Appeal.[1] Leave is usually required for an appeal, either from the Supreme Court itself, which sits in a panel of three judges to hear applications for leave to appeal, or from a provincial appellate court which may give leave (though it rarely does so) to the unsuccessful party to appeal to the Supreme Court.

The Supreme Court of Canada can be asked by the government[2] to decide a question referred to it that has not arisen in any actual case. References are usually on constitutional questions, such as the validity of a particular piece of legislation. This device enables the validity of legislation to be determined as soon as it is placed in doubt and has the advantage of putting uncertainty to rest without waiting for the point to be raised in actual litigation. A drawback of the procedure, however, is that it may accentuate the political role of the court. A government can put proposed constitutional changes before the court, and compel the court to determine their constitutional validity.[3] The validity of the proposals will fall to be determined by the court without the benefit of any experience of the practical effects of the legislation, without the benefit of a concrete set of facts giving rise to a dispute to bring the issues into focus, and without the benefit of argument and consideration of the matter by lower courts. The reference procedure may sometimes compel the Supreme Court of Canada to go beyond a purely adjudicative role, and may put the court in a difficult position. If the court holds against provincial opposition that federal proposals are constitutionally valid, it will be seen as a supporter of the federal government's political position. It is no exaggeration to say that the court cannot afford to be seen to be giving that kind of support to the government of Canada. If the court is seen by the provinces to be biased, it cannot fulfill its necessary function as umpire of intergovernmental disputes. If, on the other hand, the court, because of these fears, should lean in the other direction, it would run the risk of frustrating possibly valid and useful legislation and distorting the shape of Canadian confederation.

Provincial dissatisfaction with the court has led to recent proposals for change in its structure. The court is composed of nine judges, three

---

1 See below, p. 114.
2 The provincial governments have a corresponding power to refer questions to the provincial courts.
3 A striking example is *Ref. re Amdt. of the Constitution of Canada (Nos. 1, 2 & 3)* (1981), 125 D.L.R. (3d) 1 (S.C.C.).

of whom must be from Quebec. By convention, three have usually been appointed from Ontario, two from the West, and one from the Maritimes. A departure from this practice occurred in 1978, when a retiring Ontario judge was replaced by a judge from British Columbia, but in 1982 the number of Ontario judges was restored to three. A Chief Justice has recently said that he does not regard the judges as in any sense representatives of regional policies. They vote according to their view of the law and their perception of justice in each case. Some years ago a proposal was made to increase the number of judges to eleven, with four from Quebec. This proposal ran the risk of straining the court's sense of collegiality and common purpose, without satisfying Quebec, and the proposal has now (1992) disappeared from constitutional debate.

Another proposal sometimes made is that only Quebec judges should hear cases from Quebec involving points of civil law. This proposal seems superficially attractive. It seems that Quebec cases on Quebec law should be determined by Quebec judges. There are, however, objections to the proposal. Many questions arising under the Civil Code have a national dimension, making uniformity with other provinces essential, or highly desirable. Examples are cases involving civil liberties, or interprovincial and international commercial practice. A supreme tribunal is also necessary for resolving conflicts between Quebec law and federal law, or the law of other provinces.

The usual, though not invariable practice in civil law cases from Quebec has been for the court to sit as a panel of five, with three judges from Quebec. This ensures a majority of Quebec judges. It is difficult for a common lawyer to determine whether, as some civilians have suggested, Quebec law has been deleteriously affected by the influence of common law judges. In many cases the court is unanimous and judgment is delivered by a Quebec judge. If the Quebec judges are unanimous, they form a majority. Where there is a division of the Quebec judges, the two common law judges will have to take sides. If they are divided, the view of the two Quebec judges will carry the day. If both common law judges should support the minority Quebec judge, then they will form a majority. But it is not clear that this is objectionable. The point must, if the Quebec judges are divided, be one on which alternative views are reasonably tenable even by civil lawyers, and if the common law judges, having heard and considered the arguments, support one view rather than the other, it is not clear that this is harmful to Quebec law.

A significant problem in setting up a special constitution of the court for Civil Code cases would be the determination of which cases should go to which panel. Often a case raises several issues, only some of which may be questions of civil law. It may be disputed whether or not a point falls to be determined by the Civil Code, and only after argument is heard can a decision be made. The present practice raises no difficulty, because it is just that, a practice. Suppose the five-judge court sat to hear what was thought to be a Quebec case but it turned out to raise in addition, or instead, an important point of common law. It would have no difficulty in giving a decision, and there would be no doubt that the decision would be the binding decision of the Supreme Court of Canada. But once make it a constitutional requirement that the court must sit with Quebec judges alone for civil law cases, and the whole decision is thrown into doubt. If it was not in fact a "civil law" case, the court was wrongly constituted and the decision will presumably be invalid. Alternatively a full hearing will have to occur before constitution of the panel, in order to determine whether or not the case is a "civil law" case.

The present practice of the Supreme Court of Canada is not unique. In the House of Lords English judges sit on Scottish cases, and the Scottish judges sit on English cases, with results for both systems of law that are generally considered satisfactory. It has been pointed out that in a number of very important cases, Scottish judges have in fact overridden the view of English judges on points of English law.[4] The same must be true in Canada, though, so far as I know, no study has been made of the influence of Quebec judges on the common law. Certainly, in criminal law cases the Quebec judges often have a decisive influence. Of course, the criminal law is applicable throughout Canada, but no one suggests that because Canadian criminal law is based on principles of English law the Quebec judges are in any way disqualified. it is notable that, though it is proposed to exclude common law judges from civil law cases, no proposal has been made to exclude Quebec judges from common law cases. In my view, any such formal requirement of splitting the constitution of the court will lead to intractable jurisdictional problems, diminish the court's sense of collegiality, and achieve no substantial benefit for either system of law. The proposal, though first made many years ago, surfaced in 1978 partly as a political gesture, but of course it does not affect the politically controversial cases, that is, constitutional cases, which would still be heard by the full court. The proposal seems unlikely to appease any of the substantial dissatisfaction with the court, and may well do it harm.

It should be noted that under the present system the court only hears appeals on provincial law by leave. Consequently, where the question raised by a case is solely of concern to civilians, it can be expected that leave will be somewhat less readily granted. Where leave is granted it will presumably be because, in the judgment of the court, a question of national interest is involved, or for some other sufficient reason the case ought

---

4 Megarry, in *Miscellany-at-Law*, pp. 309-310 gives several examples of Scottish judges overriding the English on points of English law.

to be heard by the Supreme Court of Canada. In my view the power of the court to refuse leave to appeal is sufficient protection against undue interference with civil law.

If it is thought to be intolerably anomalous that the Supreme Court of Canada should determine questions of provincial law, another approach to reform would be to follow the American pattern whereby the Supreme Court of each State is the final arbiter of the law of that State. Each province would have its own final Court of Appeal, and leave to appeal to the Supreme Court would only be given in cases involving constitutional law, federal law, or conflicts between provincial laws. This proposal would, of course, still require hearings to determine whether questions of federal or constitutional law were involved. It would have other implications, too. There would probably be a demand for the judges of the provincial courts to be provincially rather than federally appointed, since they would become the final arbiters of provincial law. This in turn might lead to a suggestion of withdrawal from the provincial courts of questions of law based on federal statutes, since the provincial courts would then have become mere creatures of the provinces. Then there would probably be a need for a third level of appellate court in each province, so as to permit the final court to hear all important cases with a single panel of judges. Fourthly, there would probably be a need to adopt the American practice of a federal court to hear disputes between residents of different provinces. At present, if the Ontario courts reach a decision unsatisfactory to a resident of another province, the dissatisfied litigant has an appeal to the Supreme Court of Canada, that is, to a court that is also the final appellate court of his own province. Although appeal is only by leave, leave may well be granted in important cases of diversity among provinces. With the loss of that appeal there might well be a demand for a federal court to hear cases involving diversity of residence in the first instance. The present system enables the Supreme Court of Canada to establish a measure of uniformity in important matters of civil rights, for example, a defence of reasonable mistake in prosecutions for provincial offences, and the measure of damages for serious personal injuries in civil cases. A consequence of withdrawing provincial law from the Supreme Court of Canada would be a loss of this uniformity. Whether the disruptions to the system would be outweighed by the advantages of diminishing the jurisdiction of the Supreme Court of Canada may be considered doubtful. More generally, it may well be unwise to weaken the purely judicial functions of the court. The whole purpose of having a court, rather than a representative assembly, to determine constitutional questions is to take advantage of the reputation of judges for sober, wise and judicious decisions based on reasonable principles that are generally acceptable. If we withdraw, even in part, the traditional judicial functions from the court, we increase proportionately the number of occasions on which it will meet for political debate, and we are likely to weaken its sense of collegiality and its public reputation as a judicial body. If the constitutional court is stripped of its judicial functions, why appoint judges in the first place?

A commonly recurring suggestion is that the provinces should, in some way, have a say in the appointment of judges to the Supreme Court of Canada. This proposal is far more easily implemented than the ones just considered, and could be adopted without disrupting the present structure of the court. It would be comparatively simple to institutionalize the present practice of rotating judicial appointments among the various provinces, and then to give to the Lieutenant-Governor of the province from which each judge was appointed a power of veto over the appointment. One drawback to this proposal is that it would, in a sense, politicize the appointment of the judges. Provinces would look for supporters of their own interests rather than for the best possible judge. Another objection is that a balance must be maintained in the court of judges expert in constitutional law, criminal law, administrative law, and private law, and it is difficult to maintain a balance where the appointment power is dispersed. In favour of the proposal is the point that the Supreme Court of Canada cannot work at all unless it has the confidence of the provinces, and if a provincial veto over appointments will engender that confidence, it is a comparatively small price to pay.

The importance of the Supreme Court to the constitution of Canada can hardly be overstated. At a time of political instability and uncertainty, stability of the court and general respect for its decisions are essential to the continued existence of Confederation. Reconstituting the court in the hope of achieving greater political stability is a dangerous exercise. The probability is that the reconstituted court will lose even that measure of general respect and that degree of political cohesion possessed by the present court. It has already become plain that even public discussions of proposals for fundamental change in the structure of the court diminish the respect in which its decisions are held, and further reduce its ability to perform its proper functions.

FEDERAL COURT

Alongside the basic system of provincial Superior Courts exists a federal Superior Court, with a Trial Division and a Court of Appeal, with further appeal to the Supreme Court of Canada. The Federal Court system is not as fully developed as in the United States, where there is a completely separate federal system parallel to the State systems for hearing cases that depend on federal law or that involve parties from different States. In Canada the administration of justice generally is entrusted to the provinces.

The Criminal Code, for example, though a federal statute, is administered by the provincial courts. A federal court, formerly called the Exchequer Court, has always been used to deal with matters outside the territorial jurisdiction of any province, such as certain questions of admiralty law. The court has for many years also heard cases involving specialized areas of federal law including income tax, patents, immigration and customs law (but not, for example, bankruptcy law). Actions against the government of Canada are also heard by the Federal Court. So are actions arising out of the activities of federal administrative agencies. The jurisdiction of the court has been expanded by recent statutory provisions and there are unanswered questions as to their limits and as to their constitutionally permissible scope.

INFERIOR COURTS

Below the Superior Courts were formerly the County or District Courts (the judges of which were also federally appointed) but these have been amalgamated in most provinces with the superior courts. Below these courts are the provincial courts whose judges are provincially appointed. On the civil side, the small claims courts hear the smallest civil cases and provincial criminal courts (staffed by magistrates or provincial judges) hear less serious criminal cases. Some provinces have special juvenile and family courts. Procedures for appeal from decisions of the lower courts vary from province to province.

Recent changes and proposed changes in the small claims courts in some provinces raise interesting questions of principle. The small claims courts are designed to settle minor civil disputes with the minimum of formality. They are supposed to be easily accessible to every citizen. In practice they have become, to a large extent, collection agencies for small debts. Under recent legislation, in the Quebec small claims courts, corporations cannot initiate proceedings, lawyers are excluded, and there is no right of appeal. Originally, the Quebec legislation provided that the courts should apply only principles of natural justice and equity, but this notion proved unacceptable and the courts are now enjoined to follow the rules of evidence and to apply substantive law. The judge is to examine and cross-examine and to give equitable and impartial assistance to each party.

All these points raise interesting questions about the litigation process. The exclusion of corporations is designed to prevent the use of the court as a collection agency, but the effect is to require corporations to collect their debts in a higher court. This is almost never advantageous to the debtor, who is therefore permitted to move to transfer the proceedings to the small claims court. If he fails to do so, however, the judgment of a superior court will be entered against him. Since, if he is advised, he will almost always move for a transfer to the small claims court, virtually no practical benefit accrues to the individual litigant. Exclusion of corporations looks like a great stroke for the rights of the individual; in practice it is useless and positively inconvenient to him. Furthermore, most corporations are quite small business enterprises and many are one person businesses.

The exclusion of counsel again has an appearance of benefiting the individual, but it may not always do so. The large corporations will always be represented by experienced employees. Why should not the individual have the right to engage counsel to match that expertise? It is commonly thought that counsel prolong and add expense to proceedings. But is this true? The experience of many arbitrators in university hearings and in labour disputes is that competent counsel can help greatly in clarifying the issues to be determined and in acting as a buffer between the disputing parties where feelings run high.

The idea of natural justice and equity with no rules of evidence sounds attractive at first sight, but again it presents difficulties. Do individual litigants really want a decision according to the judge's vague idea of what is fair? It is just as probable that most litigants want a decision that is in accord with rationally defensible and consistent legal principles. As for rules of evidence, some rule is needed in any proceeding to exclude what is irrelevant or the proceeding will threaten to get completely out of hand.

The absence of appeal is also designed to save expense, and seems defensible provided that the jurisdiction of the court is not increased to too great a sum. One can tolerate the thought of litigants losing small sums to which they are legally entitled; the interests of summary decisions outweigh the interest in reaching the "right" legal result (of course, the right result is never guaranteed even where there is an appeal). But if the sum were large we should hesitate to take the same view. It would be a mistake to conclude from the success of the present court in Quebec that its jurisdiction could usefully be increased.

The injunction to the judge to act as counsel for both parties puts into question the whole concept of the adversary process. Our general philosophy of litigation is that if each party presents his case before an impartial tribunal the issues will be best clarified and the decision-maker will be in the best position to reach a just conclusion. The requirement that the judge act as counsel for the parties requires her to take sides at an early stage of the proceedings. It is likely that she will form the view that one side is in greater need of her assistance than the other, and, being human, she will perhaps tend to lean in that direction. The losing party, having been vigorously cross-examined as to credibility by the judge herself, is likely perhaps to think that the judge is not as fully impartial as he would have wished her to be. On the other hand, we must accept that not every dispute can command the same solemnity of procedure. It may be that the Quebec system of dealing with small claims rightly sacrifices some procedural niceties for the benefits of summary and inexpensive disposition.

JUDICIAL TITLES AND FORMS OF ADDRESS

Judges of the Superior Courts, including provincial Superior Courts, the Federal Courts and the Supreme Court of Canada, are traditionally described as Mr. Justice Smith or Madam Justice Smith, addressed in court as "My Lady" (sometimes Madam) or "My Lord", referred to in law reports and other legal writings as Smith J. (J.A. in the Court of Appeal) and formally addressed outside court as The Honourable Mr. (or Madam) Justice A. B. Smith. It is now common, however, for judges to be described as Justice Smith. In Ontario, judges of the General Division are addressed in court as "Your Honour". The Chief Justice of Canada is referred to in law reports, etc., as Lamer C.J.C., and the provincial Chief Justices are referred to as Smith C.J.O. or C.J.A. or C.J.Q.B., as the case may be. Outside court, it is not in my view appropriate to address judges as "My Lord" or "My Lady", although these forms of address are sometimes heard. Some consider that every distinguished person must be given a title, but it is perfectly respectful to address a Superior Court judge out of court as Mr. or Ms. Smith, or as Sir, Madam, or "Judge", a term of address long used by English barristers. Magistrates are addressed in court as "Your Worship" unless (as in Ontario) they are provincial judges in which case they are called "Your Honour".

ENGLISH COURTS

Many of the cases read by first-year law students are English, and a rough understanding of the English Superior Courts is essential to the Canadian student. The general Superior Court of original jurisdiction is the High Court of Justice, from which appeals lie to the Court of Appeal and from there to the House of Lords, which is the highest court (though the Supreme Court of Judicature is the formal name, not often used, for the High Court and the Court of Appeal together). The House of Lords as a court is quite distinct in practice from the House of Lords as the upper House of the Legislature. Only judges sit to hear legal cases. Formally, the House of Lords as a court is a committee of the House of Lords as a legislative body, but this has little practical significance. To all intents and purposes the judges, known as law lords, sit as a court. They sit in a committee room in the House of Lords at Westminster in a very informal setting without any court dress. They maintain some of the formalities of legislative language. The reasons for judgment are called speeches, and they will often contain the formal language of legislative debate ("I therefore move your lordships that this appeal be allowed", instead of: "I would allow this appeal").

Of particular importance to Canada is the Judicial Committee of the Privy Council, often called simply the Privy Council. This is not an ordinary English court at all, and does not hear appeals from the ordinary English courts. Although called a committee, like the appellate committee of the House of Lords, it is in effect a court. The formal language of the judgments is that of advice to the Crown ("Their Lordships therefore humbly advise Her Majesty that this appeal should be allowed"), but again this is mere form. The Crown always takes the advice. Until 1949,[5] the Privy Council was the highest Canadian court, hearing appeals from the Supreme Court of Canada and in some cases directly from the provincial courts of appeal. The pre-1949 judgments of the Judicial Committee are therefore a direct part of the fabric of Canadian law, and their effect is particularly striking in the field of constitutional law. The Judicial Committee continues to hear appeals from a number of Commonwealth countries, including New Zealand. The composition of the Judicial Committee is virtually the same as that of the House of Lords (though Commonwealth judges sometimes sit together with the English judges). The decisions of the Judicial Committee continue to be of interest in Canada. They are not, of course, binding on Canadian courts, but are afforded a respect similar to that given to decisions of the House of Lords.

Judges in the English High Court are known as Mr. or Mrs. Justice Smith (Smith J.), in the Court of Appeal as Lord Justice Smith (Smith L.J.), except for the Chief Judge of the Court of Appeal, whose name is followed by M.R. (Master of the Rolls), the Lord Chief Justice, who is Lord Smith L.C.J. (or C.J.), and the Vice Chancellor, who is Sir John Smith, V. C. Judges in the House of Lords, the law lords, are usually referred to as Lord Smith.

AMERICAN COURTS

Most State Superior Court systems have a trial court, an intermediate Appellate Court, and a State Supreme Court (confusingly called the Court of Appeals in New York). The federal court system consists of a trial court (called a District Court) and an appellate court known as a Circuit Court of Appeals, there being ten circuits (for various regions). The court is

---

5   1933 in criminal matters.

referred to by circuit number, for example, United States Court of Appeals, Second Circuit, abbreviated C.A.-2.

The State Supreme Courts and the Circuit Courts of Appeals are the courts of last resort in ordinary cases. The appellate jurisdiction of the United States Supreme Court is a complex matter, but the effect is that the Supreme Court can review cases of exceptional public importance, usually constitutional cases.

11

THE LEGAL PROFESSION

LAWYERS AND THE PUBLIC

From Dick's "The first thing we do, let's kill all the lawyers"[1] to the inevitable after-dinner joke about the lawyer whose childhood ambition was to be a pirate ("Congratulations!"), the legal profession has never enjoyed great popularity. This is no doubt because the lawyer is rarely the supplier of anything pleasant. Legal services never seem to produce a tangible benefit. In civil litigation the loser generally regards his lawyer's fee as the addition of insult to injury. The winner always regards herself as the recipient of simple justice, and resents having to pay a fee for what is, after all, rightfully her own. The successful criminal lawyer may enjoy some reputation in Kingston Penitentiary, but to the public at large he seems to be a threat to public security who is apt to set free dangerous criminals on what everyone knows are mere technicalities. The drawer of wills, the conveyor of real property, the administrator of estates all seem to belong to a parasitic breed who make unnecessarily complex the simple affairs of life in order to benefit themselves and the fellow members of their profession. The only clients who really appreciate the legal services they receive are hard-headed business persons who know the value of good advice about corporate organization, income tax, or labour relations. No wonder corporate practice is so popular.

The organized legal profession claims to be the guardian of the public interest. Certainly it is rigorous in dealing with dishonesty in the profession, though less so with incompetence. The organized profession is quick to suppress unauthorized practice by non-members. This is done ostensibly to protect the public from incompetence, but one need not be unduly cynical to think that the profession is also concerned to protect its monopoly,

---

1 2 Henry VI, IV, ii, 86.

especially in fields like divorce and real property conveyancing. All jurisdictions have rules restricting the entry of lawyers qualified elsewhere. Lawyers from other Canadian provinces can transfer to Ontario, for example, with some inconvenience and expense. Commonwealth and American lawyers may be required to take all or part of the curriculum at a Canadian law school.

In general, the professional legal governing bodies have acted as much in the public interest as the corresponding bodies in other professions, and it has not been shown that any other system would give the public a better profession. The principle of self-government has been modified to some extent by the inclusion, in Ontario, for example, of lay members on the governing body. It is not clear that it would be in the public interest to move in the direction of public regulation, a system that has its own drawbacks.

VARIETIES OF PRACTICE

It is a mistake to imagine that legal practitioners all do similar things. A general practice would consist largely of real estate, wills, estates, family law, incorporation of small companies, some income tax advice to individuals and small businesses, and some minor civil and criminal litigation. In large cities lawyers are to be found who specialize in each of these fields, together with some who specialize in fields such as international corporate and tax planning, admiralty law, estate planning, bankruptcy, municipal law, labour law, and patents, trademarks, and copyright law. Experts in corporate law tend to be members of large firms. Criminal lawyers, on the other hand, are often sole practitioners. Some lawyers specialize in dealing with the legal problems of the poor, in particular, the law relating to residential tenancies, immigration and social welfare.

LAWYERS OUTSIDE PRIVATE PRACTICE

There are several kinds of employment for lawyers outside private practice. Every level of government, from a medium-sized municipality to the government of Canada, employs lawyers to advise it on a whole variety of legal problems. Lawyers are employed by the provincial and federal levels of government as counsel to prosecute criminal cases on behalf of the Crown. Large corporations employ lawyers, sometimes known as "in-house counsel", to advise on all sorts of legal problems and to make submissions to appropriate bodies on legislative changes.

Law teaching should not be forgotten, and in the future lawyers may possibly be required to teach not only at university law schools but at the undergraduate university level and in high schools.

Some lawyers find employment in the business world, or in civil service departments where they do not directly make use of their legal training. The proportion of law school graduates going into the practice of law is far higher in Canada than in either England or the United States. The Canadian pattern reflects the demand for lawyers which has, until very recently, exceeded the supply. In the future, however, as the profession becomes more crowded, it is likely that a higher proportion of law school graduates will find employment in non-legal fields. This does not mean that they will regard their legal education as wasted. A good legal education is worth having for its intellectual discipline, its inherent interest, and for the understanding it gives of legal institutions.

APPOINTMENT TO THE BENCH

In civil law countries (not Quebec) a young lawyer can set out to become a judge, starting from the lowest levels of the judiciary and rising in rank as his career progresses. In Canada, however, judges are appointed from the ranks of experienced practitioners. Superior Court judges are appointed by the government of Canada, and inferior court judges by the provincial governments. Governments have, regrettably, allowed political considerations to influence judicial appointments, but there are some signs that this practice is diminishing, though it has not been eliminated. It is surely indefensible for a government to appoint a person to the bench on any basis except merit.

THE ADVERSARY SYSTEM

The system of judicial decision-making described in earlier chapters depends very heavily on each party being adequately advised and represented. Justice on both the civil and criminal sides is thought generally to be best achieved by a system in which each party, through an advocate, puts forward the strongest case that he can. Procedural rules are designed to see that each party gets a fair hearing. The role of the judge is not to discover what he may conceive to be "the truth" but to act as an impartial arbiter. It is often said, without apology, that litigation is a game played according to rules of which the judge is umpire.

Professor Glanville Williams has described this attitude as "regrettable"[2] and there are few judges who would choose today to refer in public

---

2 Williams, *Learning the Law* (8th ed.), p. 22.

to the judicial process in gaming metaphors. It is all too plain that the losers are apt to be the litigants, and not the members of the legal profession, those on the bench or those at the bar. The attitude has changed to some extent, and a judge will generally strain to avoid deciding a case on the basis of a technicality such as an error in formal pleadings.

Nevertheless, the tradition of judicial impartiality survives and can be defended. What at first sight seems a technicality may conceal an important principle. Suppose an accused person is acquitted. One who knows he committed the act charged may say: "He was guilty as sin but he got off on a technicality." "What technicality?" you ask. The answer turns out to be that the victim of the assault with which the accused was charged, the only prosecution witness, failed to appear. From one point of view, this is a miscarriage of justice (a "guilty" person goes free). From another point of view, the decision upholds an important principle, namely, that before criminal sanctions are imposed the person accused must be convincingly shown to have been guilty. Would we really want a system where the presumption of innocence is abandoned and conviction ensues without proof? Acquittal of some "guilty" persons is, most of us think, a price worth paying for maintaining the presumption of innocence and the prosecution's burden of proof. It becomes clear then that it is a little too facile to say that the court should always discover the truth, for there is more than one kind of truth.

ETHICS OF ADVOCACY

The question most often asked by the lay person of the lawyer is: "How can you defend a person you know to be guilty?" One answer to this ancient question was given by Dr. Johnson:

Boswell: But what do you think of supporting a cause which you know to be bad?

Johnson: Sir, you do not know it to be good or bad till the judge determines it. I have said that you are to state facts fairly; so that your thinking, or what you call knowing a cause to be bad, must be from reasoning, must be from your supposing your arguments to be weak and inconclusive. But, Sir, that is not enough. An argument which does not convince yourself may convince the judge to whom you urge it: and if it does convince him, why then, Sir, you are wrong, and he is right. It is his business to judge; and you are not to be confident in your own opinion that a cause is bad, but to say all you can for your client, and then hear the judge's opinion.

Boswell: But, Sir, does not affecting a warmth when you have no warmth, and appearing to be clearly of one opinion when you are in reality of another opinion, does not such dissimulation impair one's honesty? is there not some danger that a lawyer may put on the same mask in common life, in the intercourse with his friends?

Johnson: Why no, Sir. Everybody knows you are paid for affecting warmth
           for your client; and it is, therefore, properly no dissimulation: the
           moment you come from the Bar you resume your usual behaviour.
           Sir, a man will no more carry the artifice of the Bar into the common
           intercourse of society, than a man who is paid for tumbling upon
           his hands will continue to tumble upon his hands when he should
           walk on his feet.[3]

Dr. Johnson's point is that when you say you "know" a person is guilty,
you usurp the function of the court. If you put up a successful defence,
then he is not guilty in law.

This line of argument is persuasive where there is a legal defence.
A person is charged with stealing abandoned beer bottles from a park.
He admits the act. He may think he is guilty, but there may be a defence,
namely that his acts do not in law constitute theft. Again, consider the
case of the prosecution witness who fails to appear. There is no incon-
sistency in a lawyer, knowing that her client committed the act charged,
submitting that as a matter of law he cannot be convicted in the absence
of proof.

The difficult case is where the only defence is on facts that the client
frankly admits are untrue. "I committed the robbery, but I shall set up
a false alibi based on perjured evidence." There is no getting away from
the fact that this puts the lawyer in an awkward position. The lawyer has
a duty of confidentiality that absolutely prevents her from revealing the
incriminating information. The lawyer also has a duty not to mislead the
court, and it is generally agreed that she cannot call a witness, either the
accused or any other witness, to give evidence that she knows to be false.
Here, the lawyer's duty to her client stops and her duty to the court begins.
In the rather grandiose words of an Irish judge:

> This court in which we sit is a temple of justice; and the advocate of the
> Bar as well as the judge upon the Bench are equally ministers in that temple.[4]

Opinions differ on the proper course for the lawyer to follow. Some
say she should withdraw and advise her client to find another lawyer. The
objection to this is that the client is then being advised not to be so honest
with his second lawyer. Others say that the lawyer should continue with
the case, but not call the accused to give evidence. The objection to this
is that such a course will commonly result in a conviction, for the judge
or jury may assume that the reason the accused does not give evidence
is that he has not a very convincing story to tell. If the accused does not
appreciate this risk, the lawyer is setting a deadly trap by continuing the

---

3 *Boswell's Life of Johnson,* (1874 ed.), Ch. 19, pp. 155-6.
4 Crampton J. in *R. v. O'Connell* (1844), 7 Ir. L.R. 261 at 312.

case. In my opinion, the right solution is for the lawyer to explain the whole situation to the client, and, if asked for advice, to give her honest opinion. This may sometimes be that the client would be more likely to be acquitted if he engaged another lawyer who remained ignorant of the truth. If this is the lawyer's opinion, she should give it to her client. Admittedly, this may encourage the client to lie to his second lawyer but, speaking for myself, I prefer this consequence to that of the lawyer leading her client to put his head in the noose by adopting tactics that may be taken by the court as a virtual admission of guilt, at least unless the client fully appreciates the risk. As a U.S. court said:

> It would be a dark day in the history of our judicial system if a conviction is permitted to stand where an attorney . . . candidly admits that his conscience prevented him from effectively representing his client . . .[5]

The duty not to mislead the court is taken very seriously. In an English case a barrister in conducting the defence of a police officer being civilly sued for assault, put his client in the witness box in plain clothes and addressed him throughout as "Mr. Fleming" in order to conceal from the plaintiff and from the court the officer's demotion (as the result of a different incident from the one being litigated) from the rank of Chief Inspector to that of Sergeant. He also failed to correct the obvious assumption of the judge and opposing counsel that the defendant continued to hold the rank of Chief Inspector.[6] Many would say that this was a borderline case. After all, if the barrister had revealed the damaging information about his client's demotion and consequently lost the case, might the client have had a just complaint against the barrister? Nevertheless, the barrister's conduct was severely criticized by the Court of Appeal and was held by the Benchers of the Barrister's Inn of Court to be unprofessional. He was suspended from practice with very serious adverse consequences to his professional career.

Prosecuting counsel in a criminal case must put his duty to justice before his interests in securing a conviction. An American judge said that a prosecuting counsel:

> is the representative not of an ordinary party to a controversy but of a sovereignty whose obligation to govern impartially is as compelling as its obligation to govern at all, and whose interests, therefore, in a criminal prosecution, are not that it shall win a case, but that justice shall be done. As such, he is in a peculiar and very definite sense the servant of the law, the twofold aim of which is that guilt shall not escape [n]or innocence suffer.[7]

---

5 Hoffman D.J. in *Johns v. Smith*, 176 F. Supp. 949 at 954 (U.S. Dist. Ct., 1959).
6 *Meek v. Fleming*, [1961] 2 Q.B. 366 (C.A.).
7 Sutherland J. in *Berger v. U.S.*, 295 U.S. 78 at 88 (1935).

No self-respecting counsel will permit her client to dictate the exact manner in which her duties are to be performed. If a client attempts to dictate what witnesses are to be called and what questions are to be asked of them, his counsel will usually refuse to continue with the case. A nineteenth-century judge said counsel should be his client's advocate, but not his agent[8].

The barrister's oath includes promises to "neglect no man's interest" and not to refuse "causes of complaint . . . reasonably founded." In practice lawyers often refuse to undertake cases outside their own area of expertise or interest, or that they think may involve them in a conflict with duties to other clients. In a 1979 case,[9] Krever J. said that it was doubtful whether it had ever been the universally accepted understanding of a lawyer's duty in Ontario that he was bound to accept any client. The promise to refuse no cause is interpreted to mean that a lawyer is not to set himself up as judge of the merits of cases, for this might have the effect of depriving accused persons of a defence. In a well-known passage Erskine asserted the right of every accused person, however unpopular, to a legal defence:

> I will for ever, at all hazards, assert the dignity, independence, and integrity of the English Bar; without which impartial justice, the most valuable part of the English Constitution, can have no existence. — From the moment that any advocate can be permitted to say, that he *will* or *will not* stand between the Crown and the subject arraigned in the court where he daily sits to practise, from that moment the liberties of England are at an end. — If the advocate refuses to defend, from what *he may think* of the charge or of the defence, he assumes the character of the judge; nay, he assumes it before the hour of judgment; and in proportion to his rank and reputation, puts the heavy influence of perhaps a mistaken opinion into the scale against the accused, in whose favour the benevolent principle of English law makes all presumptions, and which commands the very judge to be his counsel.[10]

INFLUENCE OF ADVOCACY

Something of the influence that counsel can have may be gathered from an examination of the *Truscott* case. Truscott was a fourteen-year-old boy convicted of raping and murdering a young girl whose body was found lying in the bush near Clinton, Ontario. The evidence against Truscott was circumstantial. He was the last person known to have seen the girl alive. Truscott's story was that he had accompanied the girl to a highway, left her there, and saw her later picked up by a car which he described as a Chevrolet with yellow licence plates. Against him were three main

---

8 Pollock C.B. in *Swinfen v. Lord Chelmsford* (1860), 2 L.T. 406 at 411.
9 *Demarco v. Ungaro* (1979), 95 D.L.R. (3d) 385 at 406 (Ont. H.C.).
10 *R. v. Paine* (1792), 22 St. Tr. 357 at 412.

points. First, it was alleged that from where Truscott said he was standing it was impossible to discern the make or licence plates of a car. A photograph was intoduced at the trial taken from the place where Truscott said he was standing, and it was impossible from the photograph to distinguish the car on the highway, let alone its make or licence number. The implication was that Truscott must have been lying. Second, there was medical evidence that lesions on his penis might have been caused by rape. Thirdly, there was medical evidence that the state of the stomach contents of the dead girl showed that she must have been killed at an early time when only Truscott could have killed her. Truscott was sentenced to death, but the sentence was commuted. Subsequently, a book was written by Isobel Lebourdais that cast substantial doubt on the accuracy of the verdict.[11] Public opinion was such that the government ordered a special reference to the Supreme Court of Canada to determine whether that court would have allowed an appeal had one been made in time.

Mr. G. Arthur Martin, Q.C., now a judge of the Ontario Court of Appeal, was briefed to argue Truscott's case. As to the photograph, one does not need to be an expert in optics to realize that a photograph is very unreliable evidence of the extent and accuracy of human vision. Mr. Martin carried out a carefully prepared test. On a sunny evening, at the same time of year as the original events, he procured a 1959 Chevrolet car with yellow licence plates and parked it where Truscott said he had seen a car. Independent observers were employed to stand where Truscott said he was, and to record their observations. All could distinguish the make of the car (it was a distinctive model and cars were a special interest of Truscott's). Most could distinguish the colour of the licence plates. This evidence tended to show that Truscott might well have been telling the truth; it even tended to support his story, for he would hardly have risked inventing a story that might have been capable of disproof.

The second point was the penile lesions. At the trial a general medical practitioner with no special knowledge of skin diseases and no experience of rape was allowed to testify that in his opinion the lesions might have been caused by rape. Isobel Lebourdais suggests that this evidence may well have convinced the jury. On the reference Mr. Martin called a leading dermatologist who testified very convincingly that lesions of the sort found on Truscott's penis could not, in his view, possibly have been caused by rape, and were probably caused by some disease similar to a cold sore.

The third issue was the state of the stomach contents of the dead girl. The evidence at the trial had been that the undigested state of the stomach contents showed that the girl had met her death within two hours of her last meal. If true, this was fatal to Truscott's case. On the reference

---

11 *The Trial of Steven Truscott*, Popular Library, 1966.

the Crown called a leading expert on forensic medicine. In preparation for cross-examination, Mr. Martin had the medical librarian of Northwestern University research every article and every book ever written on establishing the time of death from stomach contents. The witness, a Dr. Simpson, had himself written a book on forensic medicine and was the editor of a leading text, namely *Taylor's Medical Jurisprudence*. Here is a part of Mr. Martin's cross-examination:

> Q: You have written extensively, Dr. Simpson, in the field of forensic medicine.
>
> A: Yes.
>
> Q: Now, I have read a good many of your books and one of the books you have written is entitled *Forensic Medicine*, and as my learned friend Mr. Scott says it has gone through five editions now.
>
> A: Yes.
>
> Q: And in the last edition indeed you say that this edition has been combed to ensure it is abreast of the times. I notice at page 7 of the book, of course I realize here that you are dealing here with a *post mortem* event, you say under the head of 'Cooling' this: "This is the only real guide to the lapse of time during the first eighteen hours after death and an early measurement is often vital to the establishment and approximate time of death."
>
> A: Yes, Sir.
>
> Q: Do you anywhere in this book say that the stomach contents and the state to which digestion has proceeded following the last meal is a reliable guide to the time of death?
>
> A: No, Sir. I think that that is, as may be evident to you, a short book for the student.
>
> Q: It would not have made it much bigger to put in a sentence indicating that the stomach contents were also a reliable guide.
>
> A: No, Sir. I appreciate that, but it is not intended to be a comprehensive work, of course, having been only for students.
>
> Q: It should contain the things upon which there is a greater consensus.
>
> A: I think you may expect the next edition, Sir, to contain . . .
>
> Q: You are going to change the next edition?
>
> A: I think it is how one improves one's textbooks, by experience.
>
> Q: When did you decide to change the next edition?
>
> A: Each time I am writing I am learning and each case helps me to improve the next edition.
>
> Q: I will throw this away and buy the next edition. . . . You also deal with this in your twelfth edition of *Taylor*, which you have edited.
>
> A: Yes, Sir.
>
> Q: I should say you do deal with the stomach contents.
>
> A: There is a reference to the stomach contents there. It is a more comprehensive book.
>
> Q: I think, to be fair, I should read everything that is there so I will not be taking it out of its context. The heading is 'Inferences as to the Time of Death'. It is page 210.
>
> A: I think I know the paragraph you are referring to.

Q: "Inferences as to the time of death in the state of food. The sight and state of digestion of contents of the stomach and bowels may be used as an additional means for fixing the hour of death in relation to the last meal. Most elaborate tables have been prepared of the time taken by the stomach to digest certain articles of diet but these are wholly unreliable."

A: Could I stop there for a moment, if it will not interfere?

Q: No, it will not interfere.

A: I would draw a sharp distinction between the state of digestion which is a chemical process and the emptying of the stomach. The state of digestion means the chemical process of digestion. I make a sharp distinction between these words.

Q: I will come to something that is relevant. "Gastric and intestinal activity is much retarded in cases of trauma and insensibility. Even without the paralysis of movement that is common to grave injury or deep insensibility the process of emptying the stomach may be very much delayed."

A: Yes, Sir.

Q: I am talking of something that is germane.

A: Yes, that's very apt.

Q: That's very apt?

A: Yes.

Q: You quote that an examination of the body of a woman strangled about 11 p.m. one February showed meat fibre, intact peas, fragment of mint leaf and potato together with some apple pips still present in the stomach. Very little had passed into the duodenum and none into the jejunum. She had had her last major meal of roast lamb, peas, boiled potatoes, mint sauce, apple tart and custard at 2:00 to 2:30 p.m. no less than nine hours previously.

A: Yes, I remember that case.

Q: The description is remarkable. First of all the cause of death was strangling.

A: Yes.

Q: The cause of death in this case was strangling and the description of the stomach contents is remarkably like the description given by Dr. Penniston [the witness for the Crown at the first trial] because it is said his examination showed meat fibre, intact peas (and intact peas I think were found here) and fragments of mint leaf and potato (and in this case Dr. Penniston felt that he could not identify the material as potatoes because it had passed into a discrete phase, although Dr. Brooks I think in fairness said he could see some pieces of potato). Do you agree that the description is very much like Dr. Penniston's?

A: Yes.

Q: Very little had passed into the duodenum; again that is remarkably like Dr. Penniston's.

A: Yes.

Q: The process seems to have gone further in the case of the deceased, Lynn Harper, because he used the words: "Very little has passed through the duodenum." Is that correct? The process was farther along than this nine hour case. Is that correct?

A: Yes.

Q: You have these analogies in the two cases and "She had her last major meal of roast beef, peas, boiled potatoes, mint sauce, apple tart and custard no less than nine hours previously."

A: Yes.[12]

The dramatic excitement of this cross-examination is still vivid to one who merely reads the written transcript.[13]

On the three key issues, visibility of the car, the penile lesions, and the stomach contents, it is thorough preparation that is the key to the advocate's success. Another example illustrating the importance of preparation, again from the criminal law, is the case of Ken Roberts, a man convicted of murdering a fellow resident in his apartment building. The main evidence against him at his trial was expert evidence that hair found near the dead woman's body matched Roberts' own hair. This evidence was based on a visual examination of the hair samples through a microscope. Roberts was convicted, and had spent three years in prison, before an expert was found who examined the hair samples by means of a much more sophisticated and accurate technique, as the result of which he was willing to say that in his opinion the hair samples could not have been from the same person. The Ontario Court of Appeal ordered a second trial, at which the evidence of the more sophisticated analysis was introduced, and Roberts was acquitted. Counsel for Roberts at his second trial was Mr. Morris Manning and, as with Mr. Martin in the *Truscott* case, the key to his success was thorough preparation. Successful counsel has to be willing to make himself an expert in optics, in skin lesions, in the state of stomach contents, on analysis of hair samples, on any subject under the sun that may be relevant to his client's case.

It is with mixed feelings that I read of these cases. There is a disturbing element in the thought that the jury in the original trials may well have been misled by medical evidence that sounded more convincing than it was. Isobel Lebourdais in her book on the *Truscott* case says that the medical evidence for the Crown was given in a confident manner and, in her opinion, it was very influential on the jury. The same seems to have been true in the *Roberts* case, where the jury was left with the false impression that the methods of analysis used were the most reliable available. There is some consolation in the thought that counsel are available of the calibre of the two mentioned in this chapter who have the capacity and the ability to rebut such false inferences. But not every accused can employ the best counsel; not every accused has the resources to carry out sight tests and to research medical libraries. It is a little disturbing to realize that courts, even criminal courts in cases of first degree murder, will be misled, that

---

12 Unpublished lecture at University of Toronto, 1972.
13 Nevertheless, the Supreme Court decided against Truscott on the reference.

they will bring in wrongful convictions, that the quality of the defence that an accused person can put up will vary from the superb to the very weak, and that the quality of the defence may influence the outcome of the cases. The legal aid system tries, but can never completely succeed, to eliminate the effects of limited financial resources on the ability of clients to employ the best counsel.

And yet, what alternative system would we have? Shall we deprive the accused of the right to the best defence he can make because everyone cannot make such a defence? On balance, the account of these cases leaves me with a sense of satisfaction. There is satisfaction in the thought that we are not yet entirely at the mercy of experts, however eminent. Reasoned dispassionate examination of the evidence by impartial non-experts can show the experts to be wrong and there still is hope for the dream of Western Society, as Professor Willis called it, of a life governed by reason.[14] The legal profession is an important part of that dream.

ORGANIZATION OF THE PROFESSION

The profession in England is divided into barristers, who only appear in court and give opinions, and solicitors (formerly called attorneys[15]) who deal generally with the legal problems of the public. In all the common law provinces in Canada, the profession is fused. Every lawyer is both a barrister and a solicitor. The admission ceremony in Ontario is still in two parts in recognition of this dual status, but otherwise the distinction is unimportant.

The chief advantage claimed for the English system is that it creates a close-knit, tightly controlled and expert bar. Canadian judges have recently been heard to complain of the quality of advocacy in the courts and it is true that in Canada a lawyer, the bulk of whose practice consists of conveying real estate, or drawing wills, can, if she wishes, walk into a Provincial Court of Appeal or the Supreme Court of Canada with little or no previous experience. It may be that as the profession becomes more crowded this will happen more often. There is no doubt that the special tradition of the English bar leads to a very high standard of advocacy and conduct in superior courts. But it is doubtful whether a divided bar would be feasible in Canada, where the administration of justice is necessarily less centralized than in England. There are, of course, Canadian lawyers who specialize in litigation, and who consider themselves heirs to the tradition of the English bar. Even they, however, deal with aspects

---

14 See above, p. 5.

15 The term "attorney", still in use in the United States, is said to have dropped out of use in England because of its inextricable association with the adjective "pettifogging".

of the litigation process that in England would fall within the province of a solicitor.

Each province has a governing body — in Ontario it is called the Law Society of Upper Canada — which is run by a group of unpaid elected "Benchers". In Ontario the Benchers include a small number of lay members appointed by the government. The legal profession is self-governing and, on the whole, the Benchers have had a good record in controlling dishonest conduct among lawyers. No lawyer takes the Discipline Committee lightly, and fraudulent lawyers are promptly disbarred. It is, however, debatable whether the record is so good in relation to professional incompetence. On the whole, the law societies have not seriously attempted to control careless or incompetent lawyers. Of course, there are serious difficulties in attempting to judge competence in a way that is useful to the public and fair to the individual lawyer. But voices are now being heard urging that the public can justifiably expect at least some sort of minimal control over competence. In those provinces where the law society runs a universal liability insurance scheme (as in Ontario) it may be that actuarial pressures will eventually compel some sort of control over those whose conduct is apt to cause large losses. Thus, communiques from the Benchers of the Law Society of Upper Canada have suggested that every lawyer should be required to keep a system to remind himself of limitation periods (time limits for bringing actions) and should be required to keep notes of title searches in real estate transactions. Missed limitation periods and careless title searching are the main causes of liability of lawyers to their clients, and so the main causes of loss to the insurance fund and indirectly to the law society and to the legal profession as a whole. It appears that one of the collateral benefits of the law society's insurance scheme will be increasing attention to standards of professional competence.

SPECIALIZATION

Many lawyers, especially in the large cities, do in practice specialize. It is becoming difficult to keep up with developments in more than a few areas. For several years there has been considerable controversy about accreditation of specialists.

If specialization exists in practice, why not permit it to be advertised? Would it not benefit the public if the information were made freely available? There are some difficulties, however. The most obvious areas of specialization are those where information is least needed. In fields such as admiralty, patents, labour law, and international tax, those seeking legal services are already in possession of the information they need. Fields in which the general public requires legal services are real estate conveyancing, wills, estates, family law, criminal law, landlord and tenant law, immigration law, consumer protection, litigation, and simple corporate and income tax planning. In a profession that is now overcrowded every newly called lawyer would want to call herself a specialist in all those fields. In the absence of a rigorously enforced system of specialist examination and accreditation the designation "specialist" is positively misleading. The law societies face some difficulties in administering a system of specialist accreditation. It cannot be deduced that the experts in any field are those that spend most time at it. Many lawyers spend a large proportion of their time conveying real estate, but this does not mean that they necessarily have a high degree of expertise in complex aspects of real estate law. It would be ironic if the routine conveyancer were entitled to be called a real estate specialist, whereas the real expert was not, because he was also an expert in a dozen other subjects as well.

The law societies would like to permit specialization, but their dilemma is that they cannot do so without either permitting lawyers to mislead the public or setting up a complex system of accreditation that would be costly to administer, might well be unfair to individual lawyers, and might still result in public confusion. What is really needed is not so much a system of specialization as a system whereby a lawyer can indicate to the public what kinds of cases he is willing to accept without claiming any special expertise in those areas. ("Not excluded from my practice: real estate, wills, family law.") The ingenuity of the profession should be sufficient to find a word for this concept. The Law Society of Upper Canada after introducing, and later abandoning, a scheme of "preferred areas of practice" now permits "specialization" in certain areas, limited at the time of writing (1992) to four.

A title that is undoubtedly confusing to the public is that of Q.C. (Queen's Counsel). Originally, the title was awarded as an honour to those barristers who were considered worthy to argue cases for the Crown. In England the title is still only given to barristers, but in Canada it is awarded to solicitors who have never argued a case in court, to law teachers, and even to politicians who have no more than nominal membership in the legal profession. Certain formal privileges survive, such as the right to wear a silk gown and to argue cases from within the bar in court (that is, from a position closer to the judge). But by and large, in Canada it has become a mere honorary appendage, indicating little more than a certain degree of seniority and a certain degree of acceptability to the government that has awarded the title. Periodically voices are heard calling for the abolition of the title, and in 1985 the Government of Ontario discontinued new awards in that province, without, however, affecting existing holders of the title.

LEGAL AID

A perpetual thorn in the side of the legal profession has been the problem of providing legal services to clients who cannot afford to pay for them. It is admitted by everyone in principle that justice should not vary according to wealth, but implementation of the principle still poses difficulties. Before 1966 in Ontario, the law society operated a voluntary legal aid scheme by virtue of which most of those charged with serious criminal offences received the services of a lawyer, often, it must be said, a very good lawyer. In 1966 Ontario introduced a provincial legal aid scheme administered by the law society but funded by the province. Under this scheme a client applies for a legal aid certificate, and contributes to the cost according to his means. Armed with the certificate, he goes to the lawyer of his choice who is paid 75 per cent of a scale of fees agreed upon by the government and the law society. The advantages of the scheme over the old voluntary system are that it removed the flavour of charity from legal aid, it makes legal aid widely available for less serious criminal offences, for civil actions, and for divorce and matrimonial disputes, it provides some assistance to persons of moderate means as well as to the destitute, and it enables the client to choose her own lawyer and to be treated by her lawyer on more or less equal terms with paying clients.

Despite its advantages, the Ontario scheme has not been without its critics. The main criticisms have been that it is administratively inconvenient to clients, and that it is too expensive to the public. It is said that the public can obtain better value for money by employing lawyers on a full-time basis to act for the indigent, rather than by paying on a fee-for-service basis. The kind of legal aid scheme staffed by full-time lawyers is often called a "public defender" system. Against the advantages of economy that such a scheme would introduce, must be set some disadvantages. One is that clients would be deprived of a choice of legal counsel. Another is a loss of independence; where judge, prosecutor, police, court officials, etc. are all government employees, there is some danger in setting up a system that makes defence counsel also a government employee. Further, there is a danger of government influence over the conduct of particular cases in a public defender system, as for example, by a hint that the taxpayers will not approve of the spending of public money on excessively lengthy or excessively technical defences, especially for persons who are clearly guilty.

The gaps in the existing legal aid scheme have been filled to some extent by legal aid clinics, staffed mainly by law students. These clinics have served a very valuable purpose in making legal help and advice easily accessible to those in need of it. The legal aid clinics have built up great expertise and many offer first-class service in such areas as immigration, landlord and tenant, consumer protection and minor criminal offences.

FEES FOR LEGAL SERVICES

Until recently, lawyers had tariffs, or schedules of fees for standard transactions. In the case of transactions involving property, such as real estate conveyancing or administration of estates, these fees were based on a percentage of the value of the property. Thus they did not represent necessarily a fair charge for the time spent on any particular transaction. It was often objected that tariffs led to overcharging, but the tariff system was defended as a convenient way of spreading fees among clients on the basis roughly of ability to pay, and on the basis that it protected clients from arbitrary overcharging. More recently, however, the tariff system has been attacked as a restraint on competition, and fixed mandatory tariffs for legal services are now less common.

The lawyer is, therefore, supposed to charge mainly on the basis of time spent on the transaction. This will vary with the seniority of the lawyer. Despite the abolition of tariffs the fee is bound to take some account of the value of the transaction to the client, and of the value of the property involved. A client who complains of a lawyer's fee can have the fee "taxed", that is, scrutinized by a court official to determine whether the fee is reasonable. Though the general basis is time spent by the lawyer, the taxing officer can also take into account the value of the service to the client.

CONTINGENT FEES

A contingent fee agreement is an arrangement between a lawyer and his client that the lawyer will be paid a proportion of the proceeds of the client's recovery in a civil action. In the United States, the contingent fee operates as a kind of legal aid system in accident cases, the lawyer normally taking thirty per cent of the winnings, and sometimes as much as fifty per cent. In Ontario, contingent fees are prohibited, as they are in England. They are, however, allowed in the majority of Canadian provinces.

In the United States, the pattern of accident litigation is very different from that in Canada. Jury trials are usual, and huge awards of damages are not uncommon. In Canada, jury trials are rarer and damage awards are low by comparison. The contingent fee system, combined with the possibility of high damages, and therefore large rewards for successful counsel, has undoubtedly played a part in encouraging a greater readiness among American plaintiffs to litigate. There are other factors that deter a Canadian litigant, in particular, the rule that an unsuccessful plaintiff must pay the defendant's costs.[16] This will make anyone think twice before suing General Motors, and this rule probably accounts, more than the contingent fee, for the difference between Canadian and American practice. Even in Ontario, where the contingent fee is officially prohibited, it is well known and considered quite proper that the fee charged will vary with the success of the result obtained by the lawyer, and that an indigent client who is suing for personal injuries caused by an accident often cannot be realistically expected to pay her lawyer at all if the action fails. It will be seen that an element of the contingent creeps into these considerations.

PREPAID INSURANCE FOR LEGAL SERVICES

For several years in the United States groups of employees of reasonable size have been able to purchase a prepaid legal services insurance plan, and publicity was recently given to such a plan in Canada. The scheme is generally that in exchange for a premium the group members are reimbursed by the insurer for the cost of certain kinds of legal services up to a maximum figure.

An analogy with medical care springs to mind, but there are differences. No one incurs medical expenses in the course of a business or on purpose to make a profit. But legal services are commonly deliberately sought for those purposes. Any system of prepaid legal insurance must develop a method of distinguishing legal services that are deliberately sought out for profit, from those that are needed unexpectedly to avert a disaster, as are medical services. This distinction is not easy to draw, but it can be expected that insurance plans will contain restrictions and maximum claim figures, designed, roughly, to exclude legal services that contribute to a profit-making enterprise or adventure.

ADVERTISING OF FEES

There has been increasing pressure in recent years to permit lawyers to advertise their fees. The professional governing bodies have, in the past, prohibited such advertising on the grounds that it is undignified, and may lead to a decline in the quality of legal services. Against this, it is said that prohibition of advertising is a restraint on competition, that it cannot be shown that advertising leads to a decline in quality of service, and that the "dignity" of the profession is an insufficient value to set against the

---

16 Costs awarded to a successful party do not, however, amount to a complete indemnity. Such costs, called "party and party costs" usually amount to about two-thirds of the actual costs incurred. Where for some reason (e.g., strong disapproval of the plaintiff's conduct), the court wishes to award a full indemnity, it awards "solicitor and client costs".

the virtue of free competition. Several provinces now permit advertising (in a suitably dignified manner) of sample fees, and the trend appears to be toward greater freedom to advertise.

Appendix A

LATIN WORDS AND PHRASES IN COMMON LEGAL USE

A

a fortiori, with stronger reason
a mensa et thoro, from bed and board
a priori, from first principles
a vinculo matrimonii, from the bond of matrimony *(cf. a mensa et thoro)*
ab initio, from the beginning
absente reo, in the absence of the accused
abundantia cautelae non nocet, abundance of caution does no harm
actio, action
actio per quod servitium amisit, action for loss of services
actio personalis moritur cum persona, a personal action dies with the person
actus non facit reum nisi mens sit rea, an act does not make a person guilty
   unless he has a guilty mind
actus reus, criminal act
ad hoc, for this (special) purpose
ad hominem, directed to the individual person
ad idem, at one
ad infinitum, forever
ad litem, for the lawsuit
ad valorem, according to value
aequitas, equity
aequitas sequitur legem, equity follows the law
affidavit, he asserts (statement of oath)
alias, otherwise (indicating alternative name)
alibi, elsewhere (a defence to a criminal charge)
aliter, otherwise

allocutus, the demand put to a person convicted of treason or felony whether he has anything to say why sentence should not be passed

alter ego, one's other self

amicus curiae, (plural: *amici curiae*), friend of the court, a disinterested adviser

anglice, in English

animus contrahendi, intention of contracting

animus (animo) furandi, (with) the intention of stealing

animus (animo) manendi, (with) the intention of staying

animus revertendi, intention of returning

animus revocandi, intention of revoking (a will)

animus testandi, intention of making a will

ante litem motam, before litigation was initiated

arguendo, in argument

assumpsit, "he undertook", form of pleading used to enforce contractual promises

B

bona, goods

bona fide, (note: the nominative* is *fides*), in good faith

bona fides, good faith

bona mobilia, moveable goods

bona vacantia, unowned goods

C

cadit quaestio, the question falls

capias ad satisfaciendum (ca.sa.), take in satisfaction (opening words of a writ empowering the arrest of a debtor)

casus omissus, a case of omission

causa causans, causing cause

causa effectiva, effective cause

causa sine qua non, indispensable cause

caveat, warning

caveat actor, let the doer beware

caveat emptor, let the buyer beware

caveat venditor, let the seller beware

certiorari, "to be informed" (opening words of a writ)

certum est quod certum reddi potest, that is certain that can be rendered certain

cessante ratione cessat ipsa lex, when the reason ceases, so does the law itself

ceteris paribus, other things being equal

cognovit, acknowledgement that one has no defence to an action

colore officii, by colour of office

communis error facit jus, common error makes law

compos mentis, of sound mind

consensus (ad idem), agreement (in the same terms) *consortium,* companionship

contra, against

contra bonos mores, against good morals

contra proferentem, against the proferror (*i.e.,* one who prepares a document)

coram, in the presence of

corpus delicti, substance of the offence

cuius est dare eius est disponere, he who gives can also direct the disposition of the gift

cuius est solum, eius est usque ad caelum et ad inferos, whoever owns the soil owns up to the sky and down to the centre of the earth ("to heaven and hell")

culpa, fault

curia advisari vult, the court takes time for consideration ("wishes to be advised")

D

damnum sine (or absque) injuria, loss without legal cause of action

de bene esse, conditionally

de bonis asportatis, in respect of goods carried away

de bonis non administratis, in respect of goods not administered

de facto, in fact

de jure, in law

de minimis non curat lex, the law does not care about trifles *de novo,* anew

delegatus non potest delegare, a delegate cannot delegate *dictum* (plural *dicta*), thing said

dissentiens (in absolute phrases* only, *dissentiente*), dissenting

donatio, gift

donatio mortis causa, gift in contemplation of death

dubitans, (in absolute phrases* only, *dubitante*), doubting

dum se bene gesserint, during good behaviour

dum (sola et) casta, while (single and) chaste

E

ei qui affirmat, non ei qui negat, incumbit probatio, the burden of proof lies on him who affirms, not on him who denies a fact

eiusdem generis, of the same class

eo instanti, at that instant

et alii, or et alios (accusative*), *et al.,* and others

et alius, et alium, et al., and another

et uxor (et ux), and wife

ex abundanti cautela, from excessive caution

ex aequo, equitably

ex aequo et bono, on a fair and equitable basis

ex concessis, from what has been conceded

ex contractu, founded on contract

ex curia, out of court

ex (or *e) debito justitiae,* by debt of justice

ex delicto, founded on tort

ex gratia, from kindness (*i.e.,* voluntarily)

ex improviso, unforeseeable, unforeseeably

ex (or *e) mero* (or *proprio) motu,* of his own motion

ex nudo pacto non oritur actio, no action arises from a bare promise

ex officio, by virtue of office

ex parte, on one side only

ex post facto, afterwards

ex turpi causa (or *ex dolo malo) non oritur actio,* from an evil cause no action arises

exceptio confirmat (or *probat) regulum,* the exception proves the rule

exeat, "let him go" (*i.e.,* permission to leave)

expressis verbis, in express terms

expressum facit cessare tacitum, the express displaces the implied

F

factum, act or deed

falso demonstratio non nocet, a false example does not impair the principle

felo de se, suicide

ferae naturae, of wild nature

fiat, let it be done, command

fiat justitia ruat caelum, let justice be done though the heavens fall

fieri facias (fi. fa.), cause to be done (opening words of a writ of execution)

filius nullius, bastard

fons et origo, source and origin

forum, court

forum (non) conveniens, (in)convenient forum

fraus omnia vitiat, fraud vitiates everything

fructus indistriales, industrial crops (*i.e.,* grown by industry)

fructus naturales, natural fruits

functus officio, having fulfilled an office

G

generalia specialibus non derogant, general provisions do not detract from particular

gravamen, the serious aspect or matter of something

H

habeas corpus, "you must have the body" (opening words of a writ to test the legality of imprisonment)

habendum et tenendum, to have and to hold

I

ibidem (or *ibid.*), in the same place

idem (or *id.*), the same

ignoramus, "we do not know", word formally used to reject a bill of indictment

ignorantia juris non (haud, neminem) excusat, ignorance of the law is no excuse

imperitia culpae adnumeratur, lack of knowledge is counted as fault

imperium, executive authority

in absentia, in absence

in banco, in bank (*i.e.*, the whole court sitting together)

in banco regis, in the King's Bench

in camera, in secret

in capite, in chief

in esse, in being

in extenso, extensively

in extremis, at the point of death

in fieri, in course of accomplishment

in flagrante delicto, in the very act of committing a crime; red-handed

in invitum, against an unwilling person

in limine, at the threshold

in loco parentis, in the place of a parent

in medias res, into the middle of things

in pari delicto potior est conditio defendentis (or *possidentis*), in equal fault the defendant's (or possessor's) position is the stronger

in pari materia, analogous ("in equal material")

in personam, personal (*cf. in rem*)

in posse, that which may be (but does not yet exist)

in praesenti, at present

in propria persona, in person

in re, in the matter (of)

in rem, directed to an actual piece of property *(cf. in personam)*
in situ, in its original situation
in specie, in specific form (as opposed, usually, to a monetary equivalent)
in statu quo (ante), in the original state
in terrorem, as a threat
in totidem verbis, in so many words
in toto, entirely
in transitu, in passage
in vacuo, in a vacuum
inclusio unius exclusio alterius, the inclusion of one thing is the exclusion
    of the other
incrementum, increase
indicium (plural *indicia),* sign
infra, below
injuria absque (or *sine) damno,* legal injury without actual loss
inter alia, among other things
inter alios, among other persons
inter se, among themselves, between each other
inter vivos, between living persons
interesse termini, the interest in a term *(i.e.,* a lessee's interest in land before
    taking possession)
interest reipublicae ut sit finis litium, it is in the public interest to put an
    end to lawsuits
intra vires, within the powers
ipso facto, by the very fact
ipse dixit, "he himself said" *(i.e.,* a bare assertion)
item, also

J

jurat "he swears", statement at end of affidavit showing when and before
    whom it was sworn
jus, right, law
jus accrescendi, right of accretion *(e.g.,* succession to property by joint
    tenant)
jus civile, civil law
jus gentium, the law of nations
jus naturale, natural law
jus quaesitum tertio, right asserted by a third person
jus spatiendi, right of walking about
jus tertii, the right of a third person
jus venandi et piscandi, right of hunting and fishing

L

laesio enormis, great "harm", hence, discrepancy between price and value in contract

lapsus calami, slip of the pen

lapsus linguae, slip of the tongue

lex, law

lex causae, the law of the cause

lex domicilii, the law of the domicile

lex fori, the law of the forum (*i.e.,* the domestic court)

lex loci actus, law of the place of the act

lexi loci celebrationis, law of the place of celebration

lex loci contractus, the law of the place of the contract

lex loci delicti, the law of the place of the tort

lex loci solutionis, law of the place of performance

lex non cogit ad impossibilia, the law does not compel the impossible

lex situs, law of the place (*e.g.,* of land)

lis alibi pendens, lawsuit pending elsewhere

lis pendens, a pending lawsuit (see *pendente lite)*

loco citato (loc. cit.), in the place cited

locus delicti, place of the tort

locus paenitentiae, room for repentance

locus regit actum, the place governs the act

locus standi, "place of standing", a right to be heard before a court

M

mala fide (note the nominative* is *fides),* in bad faith

mala fides, bad faith

malum (plural *mala) in se,* evil in itself

malum (plural *mala) prohibitum (a),* evil only because forbidden

mandamus, "we command" (opening words of a writ requiring performance of some act)

mansuetae naturae, of tame nature

mare clausum, closed sea (*i.e.,* within a single state)

mens rea, guilty mind

meum et tuum, mine and yours

mobilia sequuntur personam, movables follow the person

modus operandi, mode of operation

mora, delay

motu proprio, of his own accord

mutatis mutandis, with necessary changes

N

ne exeat regno, let him not depart from the realm (opening words of a writ to prevent a defendant from leaving the jurisdiction)

nec vi nec clam nec precario, neither by force, nor secretly, nor by permission

negotiorum gestio, conduct of affairs

nemo dat quod non habet, no one gives what he does not have

nemo debet bis vexari pro eadem causa, no one should be twice troubled by the same cause

nemo judex (debet esse) in sua causa, no one (should be) judge in his own cause

nemo suam turpitudinem allegans audiendus est, no one is to be heard alleging his own wrongdoing

nemo tenetur seipsum accusare (prodere), no one is compelled to incriminate (betray) himself

nihil (nil), nothing

nihil ad rem, irrelevant

nisi, unless

nisi prius, "unless before", the name of the civil assize court, originally directed to be tried in London unless before the trial an assize judge should try it on circuit

nolle prosequi, unwillingness to prosecute (*i.e.,* a formal undertaking to discontinue criminal proceedings)

nolo contendere, I do not wish to dispute (*i.e.,* an admission of guilt)

non compos mentis, of unsound mind

non est factum, it is not [my] deed

non obstante, notwithstanding

non obstante veredicto (N.O.V.), notwithstanding the verdict

non possumus, we are unable

non sequitur, it does not follow (logical fallacy)

noscitur a sociis, it is known by its associates

nota bene (N.B.), note well

novus actus interveniens, new act intervening (*i.e.,* to break a chain of causation)

nudum pactum, bare pact (*i.e.,* a promise without consideration)

nulla bona, no goods

nulla poena sine lege, no punishment without a law

nullum tempus occurrit regi, time does not run against the King

nunc pro tunc, now for then (*i.e.,* retroactively)

O

obiter, by the way

obiter dictum (plural *dicta*), thing said by the way

omnia praesumuntur contra spoliatorem, all is presumed against a wrongdoer

omnia praesumuntur rite esse acta, everything is presumed to have been properly done

onus, burden

onus probandi, burden of proof

P

pacta sunt servanda, agreements should be kept

parens patriae, father of the country

pari passu, in equal step (*i.e.,* equally)

particeps criminis, accessory to a crime

passim, throughout

pendente lite, the lawsuit pending

per, by

per annum, yearly

per caput (or *capita*), by head, or by heads

per curiam, by the court (no connection with *per incuriam*)

per incuriam, by carelessness (no connection with *per curiam*)

per saltum, by a jump

per se, by itself

per stirpes, by stocks (*i.e.,* several children divide their parent's share of property, *cf. per capita*)

persona designata, person designated or appointed for a special function

persona (non) grata, (un)welcome person

post hoc, ergo propter hoc, after this therefore because of this (logical fallacy)

post litem motam, after litigation was initiated

post mortem, after death

potior est conditio defendentis (or *possidentis*), the defendant's (possessor's) position is stronger

prima facie, at first sight

pro bono publico, for the public good

pro forma, as a matter of form

pro hac vice, for this occasion

pro rata, in proportion

pro tanto, for so much or so far

proprio motu, of its own motion

proprio vigore, by its own power

proviso, "provided", an exception or condition in a document

Q

qua, in (his) capacity as . . .
quaere, question, query
quaeritur, the question is asked
quamdiu se bene gesserint, during good behaviour
quantum meruit, how much he deserved
quantum valebat (valebant), how much it was (they were) worth
quare clausum fregit, whereby he broke the close (*i.e.,* trespassed on land)
quasi, as if
qui facit per alium facit per se, he who acts through another acts himself
qui prior est tempore potior est jure, first in time is stronger in law
qui sentit commodum sentire debet et onus, he who reaps the benefit of
   anything should bear the burden
quia timet, "because he fears" an injunction in anticipation of wrongful
   conduct
quid pro quo, something for something else, price
quis custodiet ipsos custodes?, who will guard the guards themselves?
quo jure?, by what right?
quo warranto, "by what warrant" (opening words of a writ to review the
   right of a person to hold office)
quorum, "of whom", the minimum number needed for a valid meeting

R

ratio decidendi, reason for deciding
rebus sic stantibus, things remaining as they are
Regina, queen
remanet, "it remains", case left over in a court list from a previous term
res, thing, matter, substance
res gestae, things done, facts surrounding an incident
res integra, a point that is undecided by authority
res inter alios acta, a matter transacted between others (*i.e.,* a collateral
   transaction)
res ipsa loquitur, the thing speaks for itself
res judicata, matter adjudicated
res nullius, nobody's thing
res perit domino, the owner of a thing bears the risk of its loss
respondeat superior, let the employer respond (*i.e.,* be liable)
restitutio in integrum, restoration to a former state
Rex, king
Rex non potest peccare, the king can do no wrong
rigor mortis, stiffening of death

S

sciens, knowing
scienter, knowingly
scilicet (sc), that is to say
sed quaere, but this is open to question
sic, thus
sic utere tuo ut alienum non laedas, use your own property so that you
   do not harm another
simpliciter, simply
sine die, without a day (*i.e.,* indefinitely)
sine prole, without issue
sine qua non, without which not (*i.e.,* essential)
situs, place
solatium, solace
spes, hope, expectation
sponte sua, of one's own accord
stare decisis, to stand by decisions (*i.e.,* to observe precedent)
status quo (ante), the original state
stricto sensu, in a strict sense, strictly speaking
sub nomine, under the name (of)
sub judice, before the courts
subpoena (ad testificandum), "under penalty for testifying" (opening words
   of a writ, and hence an order to appear in court)
subpoena duces tecum, "under penalty bring with you" (opening words
   of a writ requiring a person to bring evidence to court)
suggestio falsi, see *suppressio veri*
sui generis, of its own kind
sui juris, capable of managing one's own affairs
suppressio veri suggestio falsi, the suppression of truth is the suggestion
   of falsehood
supra, above

T

tabula rasa, clean slate
talem qualem, just as he happens to be
terminus ad quem, limit
tertium quid, a third something
turpis causa, evil cause

U

uberrima fides, the utmost good faith

uberrimae fidei, of the utmost good faith

ubi jus, ibi remedium, where there is a right there is a remedy

ultra vires, beyond the powers

unusquisque spondet peritiam artis suae, everyone warrants the skill of his own art

ut res magis valeat quam pereat, that the matter may rather be strengthened than perish

V

venire de novo, new trial

venire facias, cause to come (opening words of a writ to summon a jury)

verba chartarum fortius accipiuntur contra proferentem, words of documents are more strongly construed against one who profers the document

verba ita sunt intelligenda ut res magis valeat quam pereat, words are to be understood to give effect to rather than to destroy the transaction or object

verbatim, word for word

versus, against

vi et armis, by force of arms

vice versa, the other way around

vide, see

videlicet (or *viz*), to wit, namely

vigilantibus non dormientibus lex succurrit, the law aids the watchful, not the sleepy

vinculum juris, "chain of law" (*i.e.,* relevant connection)

vis major, main force

viva voce, with living voice (*i.e.,* orally)

volenti non fit injuria (note that in the nominative case* "a willing person" is *volens* not *volenti*), no legal injury occurs to one who is willing

---

* *If you neither know nor care to know about nominatives, accusatives and absolutes, stick to English.*

WORDS AND PHRASES DERIVED FROM FRENCH

A

allonge, a slip of paper annexed to a bill or note
amercement, a fine
arraign, bring before a criminal court
assize, session of a court
autrefois acquit, acquitted at another time (defence to criminal charge)
autrefois convict, convicted at another time (defence to criminal charge)

C

cesser, the end of a term (*e.g.,* of a lease)
cestui que trust, beneficiary of a trust
cestui que use, beneficiary of a use
cestui que vie, life in being
chose, thing
chose in action, right of action
chose in equity, right enforceable by proceedings in equity *cousin german,*
   first cousin
cy-près, as near as possible

D

de son tort, by his own wrong
dehors, outside
detinue, wrongful detention of property
disseisin, dispossession
distrain, distress, (take) possession of goods as security for debt owing

distress damage feasant, the right to take possession of cattle that damage land

dominant tenement, land having right over other land

E

emblements, crops
eminent domain, the right of a state to expropriate
en ventre sa mère, in his mother's womb
entail, create a fee tail
escheat, reversion of property to the Crown
escrow, condition
estop, estoppel, preclude, preclusion (of a party from making a particular assertion)

F

fait, deed
fee, estate in land
fee tail, estate in land limited to direct descendants
femme covert, married woman
femme sole, single woman
feoffment, entitlement to land
force majeur, main force, irresistible compulsion

G

grand jury, jury that used to present an indictment

H

hereditament, land that would descend to an heir

I

laches, delay
lèse majéste, treason
letters patent, "open letters" granting some licence or privilege by the sovereign

L

lien, a security interest in property
livery, delivery

M

market overt, "open market", where a buyer could be assured of good title
mesne, intermediate
misfeasance, wrongdoing
moiety, half
mortgage, "dead pledge", conveyance of land as security for a loan
mortmain, "dead hand", land holding by a corporation

N

nonfeasance, omission

O

oyez!, hear ye!

P

parol, oral
parole, word of honour, hence release of prisoner on honour
peine forte et dure, severe and hard pain (an early kind of judicial torture)
per my et per tout, by half and by whole (*i.e.*, undivided half interest)
petty jury, jury that tries a criminal case
possession vaut titre, possession warrants title
profit à prendre, right to profit from land
puisne, junior (*e.g.*, *puisne* judge)
pur autre vie, for another's life

R

renvois, sending back
replevin, recovery of goods unlawfully taken

S

sans recours, without recourse
seise (seize), take possession of
seisin, possession
semble, it seems
servient tenement, land subject to right in other land
sign manual, the sovereign's personal signature

T

tort, civil wrong
tortfeasor, one who commits a civil wrong
treasure trove, hidden money that is found
trover, "finding", hence an action to recover goods from a person not entitled
to them

V

venue, place of holding a trial
voir dire, trial within a trial to determine a subsidiary question (corruption
of *vrai dire*)

Appendix C

LAW REPORTS, DIGESTS, ENCYCLOPEDIAS, LOOSELEAF SERVICES, AND PERIODICALS

ENGLISH LAW REPORTS

Before 1866
Reports were generally known by the names of the reporters (nominate reports) and most are reprinted in a series called the English Reports (E.R.). A table of concordance to the original nominate reports is provided in every law library. Very early cases are noted in a series called Year Books.

1866-1875

The semi-official series called the Law Reports begins with eleven subseries:

- House of Lords, English and Irish Appeals (L.R. . . . H. L.)
- House of Lords, Scotch and Divorce Appeals (L. R. . . .H. L. Sc. & Div.)
- Privy Council Appeals (L.R. . . .P.C.)
- Chancery Appeal Cases (L.R. . . .Ch. App.)
- Equity Cases (L.R. . . . Eq.)
- Crown Cases Reserved (L.R. . . .C. C. R.)
- Queen's Bench Cases (L.R. . . .Q. B.)
- Common Pleas Cases (L.R. . . .C. P.)
- Exchequer Cases (L.R. . . . Ex.)
- Admiralty and Ecclesiastical Cases (L.R. . . .A. & E.)
- Probate and Divorce (L.R. . . . P. & D.)

Note: E.g. Ayerst v. Jenkins (1873), L.R. 16 Eq. 275.

1875-1880:

The number of series is reduced to six:

- Appeal Cases (App. Cas.)
- Chancery Division (Ch. D.)
- Queen's Bench Division (Q.B.D.)
- Common Pleas Division (C.P.D.)
- Exchequer Division (Ex. D.)
- Probate Division (P.D.)

Note: "L.R." is omitted from citations. *E.g., Baker v. Hedgecock* (1888), Ch. D. 520.

1881-1890:

The series are reduced to four, by the incorporation of Common Pleas and Exchequer into the Reports of the Queen's Bench Division.

1891-present

The four series continue with abbreviations as follows:

- Appeal Cases (A.C.)
- Chancery Division (Ch.)
- Queen's Bench (Q.B.) (or K.B.)
- Probate Divorce and Admiralty, renamed in 1970 Family Division (before 1971, P.; now Fam.)

Note that since 1891, the volumes are numbered by their dates, not by sequential volume numbers. Square brackets are therefore used, *e.g., Angus v. Clifford,* [1891] 2 Ch. 449. There is an excellent index to the Law Reports (the "pink index"), which is kept up to date with cumulative parts, and annual and decennial consolidations.

ENGLISH UNOFFICIAL SERIES

Weekly Law Reports

The Law Reports publish a series called the Weekly Law Reports (W.L.R.), which serves two separate purposes. Volumes 2 and 3 in each year are advance publications of cases to be reported in the Law Reports. Volume I is for cases not intended to appear in the Law Reports, that is to say, cases thought to be of less importance.

Other Series

- All England Law Reports (All E.R.) (This series is indexed.)
- Commercial Cases (Com. Cas.)
- Common Market Law Reports (C.M.L.R.)
- Cox's Criminal Cases (Cox C.C.)
- Criminal Appeal Reports (Cr. App. R.)

- Fleet Street (Patent Law) Reports (F.S.R.)
- Industrial Cases Reports (I.C.R.)
- Justice of the Peace (J.P.)
- Knight's Industrial Reports (K.I.R.)
- Law Journal Admiralty (L.J. Adm.)
- Law Journal Bankruptcy (L.J. Bk.)
- Law Journal Chancery (L.J. Ch.)
- Law Journal Common Pleas (L.J.C.P.)
- Law Journal Crown Cases Reserved (L.J.C.C.R.)
- Law Journal Ecclesiastical (L.J. Ecc.)
- Law Journal Exchequer (L.J. Ex.)
- Law Journal House of Lords (L.J. H. L.)
- Law Journal Magistrates Cases (L.J.M.C.)
- Law Journal Privy Council (L.J.P.C.)
- Law Journal Probate Divorce & Admiralty (L.J.P.D.A.)
- Law Journal Queen's Bench (L.J.Q.B.)
- Law Times Reports (L.T.R.)
- Lloyd's Law Reports (Lloyd's Rep.)
- Lloyd's List Law Reports (Ll. L.R.)
- Local Government Reports (L.G.R.)
- Property and Compensation Reports (Prop. & Comp. R.)
- Reports of Patent Design and Trade Mark Cases (R.P.C.)
- Restrictive Practices Cases (R.P.C.)
- Road Traffic Reports (R.T.R.)
- Tax Cases (T.C.)
- Times Law Reports (T.L.R.)
- Value Added Tax Tribunal Reports (V.A.T.T.R.)
- Weekly Notes (W.N.)

ENGLISH DIGESTS AND ENCYCLOPEDIAS

- Current Law
- English and Empire Digest
- Halsbury's Laws of England (The 3rd edition, but not the 4th, has a Canadian Converter, *i.e.*, supplemental volumes for Canadian law.)

CANADIAN LAW REPORTS

The following are the most important Canadian series:

- Administrative Law Reports (Admin. L.R.)
- Alberta Law Reports (Alta. L.R.)
- Alberta Reports (A.R.)
- British Columbia Corporation Law Guide (B.C. Corps. L.G.)

- British Columbia Reports (B.C.R.)
- British Columbia Law Reports (B.C.L.R.)
- British Columbia Tax Reports (B.C.T.R.)
- Business Law Reports (B.L.R.)
- Canada Corporations Law Reports (C.C.L.R.)
- Canada Tax Cases (C.T.C.)
- Canada Tax Manual (C.T.M.)
- Canadian Bankruptcy Reports (C.B.R.)
- Canadian Cases on Employment Law (C.C.E.L.)
- Canadian Cases on the Law of Insurance (C.C.L.I.)
- Canadian Cases on the Law of Torts (C.C.L.T.)
- Canadian Commercial Law Guide (C.C.L.G.)
- Canadian Criminal Cases (C.C.C.)
- Canadian Customs and Excise Reports (C.E.R.)
- Canadian Employment Benefits and Pension Guide Reports (C.E.B. & P.G.R.)
- Canadian Employment Safety and Health Guide (C.E.S.H.G.)
- Canadian Environment Law Reports (C.E.L.R.)
- Canadian Health Facilities Law Guide (C.H.F.L.G.)
- Canadian Human Rights Reporter (C.H.R.R.)
- Canadian Insurance Law Reports (C.I.L.R.)
- Canadian Labour Law Cases (C.L.L.C.)
- Canadian Labour Relations Boards Reports (Cdn. L.R.B.R.)
- Canadian Native Law Reporter (C.N.L.R.)
- Canadian Occupational Health & Safety Cases (C.O.H.C.)
- Canadian Patent Reporter (C.P.R.)
- Canadian Railway Cases (C.R.C.)
- Canadian Railway and Transport Cases (C.R.T.C.)
- Canadian Rights Reporter (C.R.R.)
- Canadian Sales Tax Reports (Cdn. S.T.R.)
- Canadian Securities Law Reports (C.S.L.R.)
- Canadian Transport Cases (C.T.C.)
- Carswell's Practice Cases (C.P.C.)
- Construction Law Reports (C.L.R.)
- Criminal Reports (C.R.)
- Dominion Law Reports (D.L.R.) (This series has an annotation service.)
- Dominion Tax Cases (D.T.C.)
- Eastern Law Reports (E.L.R.)
- Estates and Trusts Reports (E.T.R.)
- Exchequer Court Reports (Ex. C.R.)
- Family Law Reform Act Cases (F.L.R.A.C.)
- Federal Court Reports (F.C. or C.F.)
- Federal Trial Reports (F.T.R.)

- Fox's Patent Cases (Fox Pat. C.)
- Grant's Chancery Reports (G.R.)
- Immigration Appeal Cases (I.A.C.)
- Insurance Law Reporter (I.L.R.)
- Labour Arbitration Cases (L.A.C.)
- Land Compensation Reports (L.C.R.)
- Legal Medical Quarterly (L. Med. Q.)
- Manitoba and Saskatchewan Tax Reports (Man. & Sask. Tax R.)
- Manitoba Reports (Man. R.)
- Maritime Provinces Reports (M.P.R.)
- Motor Vehicle Reports (M.V.R.)
- Municipal and Planning Law Reports (M.P.L.R.)
- National Reporter (N.R.)
- New Brunswick Reports (N.B.R.)
- Newfoundland & Prince Edward Island Reports (Nfld. & P.E.I.R.)
- Newfoundland Reports (Nfld. R.)
- Northwest Territories Reports (N.W..R.)
- Nova Scotia Reports (N. S. R.)
- Ontario Appeal Cases (O.A.C.)
- Ontario Appeal Reports (O.A.R.)
- Ontario Corporations Law Guide (O.C.L.G.)
- Ontario Labour Relations Board Reports (O.L.R.B. Rep.)
- Ontario Law Reports (O.L.R.)
- Ontario Municipal Board Reports (O.M.B.R.)
- Ontario Reports (O.R.)
- Ontario Securities Commission Bulletin (O.S.C.B.)
- Ontario Tax Reports (Ont. Tax R.)
- Ontario Weekly Notes (O.W.N.)
- Ontario Weekly Reporter (O.W.R.)
- Personal Property Security Act Cases (P.P.S.A.C.)
- Practice Reports (P.R.)
- Quebec Court of Appeal (Que. C.A. or C.A.)
- Quebec Queen's Bench (Que. Q.B. or B.R.)
- Quebec Tax Reports (Que. T.R.)
- Quebec Taxation Service (Que. T.S.)
- Quebec Superior Court (Que. S.C. or C.S.)
- Rapports de Pratique de Québec (R.P.)
- Real Property Reports (R.P.R.)
- Recueils de jurisprudence du Québec: Cour d'appel (C.A.)
- Recueils dejurisprudence du Québec: Cour provinciale (C.P.)
- Cour des Sessions de la paix (C.S.P.)
- Tribunal de la jeunesse (T.J.)
- Recueils dejurisprudence du Québec: Cour supérieure (C.S.)

- Reports of Family Law (R.F.L.)
- Reports of Patent Cases (R.P.C.)
- Revue de Droit Judiciaire (R. D.J.)
- Revue Legal (R.L.)
- Saskatchewan Law Reports (Sask. L.R. or S.L.R.)
- Saskatchewan Reports (Sask. R.)
- Supreme Court Reports (S.C.R.)
- Tax Appeal Board Cases (T.A.B.C.)
- Territories Law Reports (Terr. L.R.)
- Upper Canada Chancery Chambers Reports (U.C. Ch. Ch.)
- Upper Canada Common Pleas (U.C.C.P.)
- Upper Canada Error & Appeal Reports (U.C.E. & A.)
- Upper Canada Queen's Bench (U.C.Q.B.)
- Western Labour Arbitration Cases (WL.A.C.)
- Western Law Reporter (W.L.R.)
- Western Weekly Reports (W.W.R.)
- Workmen's Compensation Reports (W.C.R.)

CANADIAN DIGESTS, ENCYCLOPEDIAS AND INDEXES

- All-Canada Weekly Summaries (A.C.W.S.)
- Annuaire de Jurisprudence du Quebec
- Butterworth's Ontario Digest
- Canadian Abridgment
- Canadian Current Law (C.C.L.)
- Canadian Encyclopedic Digest (C.E.D.)
- Canadian Weekly Law Sheet
- Dominion Report Service
- Index Gagnon (for Quebec law)
- Supreme Court of Canada Report Service
- Weekly Criminal Bulletin

CANADIAN LOOSELEAF SERVICES

- Air Law (Showcross and Beaumont; Butterworths)
- Alberta Compensation Manual (Carswell)
- Annotated British Columbia Company Act (Cumberford; Carswell)
- Annotated Business Corporations of Alberta (Currie; Carswell)
- Annotated Insurance Act of Ontario (Weir; Carswell)
- Annotated Municipal Act of Ontario (Auerback and James; Carswell)
- Annotated Ontario Business Corporations Act (Adams; Canada Law Book)
- Appellate Practice (Butterworths)

- Art and Science of Advocacy (Olah; Carswell)
- Bankruptcy Law of Canada (Houlden and Morawetz; Carswell)
- Breathalyzer Law in Canada (Third Ed.) (McLeod, Takach and Segal; Carswell)
- British Columbia Annotated Industrial Relations Act (Russell and DuMoulin; Butterworths)
- British Columbia Corporations Law Guide (C.C.H.)
- British Columbia Corporations Manual (Carswell)
- British Columbia Practice (McLachlin and Taylor; Butterworths)
- British Columbia Tax Reporter (C.C.H.)
- British Columbia Taxation Service (Carswell)
- Business Legal Adviser (Rossiter; Carswell)
- Canada Corporations Law Reporter (C.C.H.)
- Canada Corporations Manual (Carswell)
- Canada Income Tax Guide (C.C.H.)
- Canada Labour Relations Board (Clarke; Canada Law Book)
- Canada Labour Service (Carswell)
- Canada Regulations Index (Carswell)
- Canada Tax Services (Carswell)
- Canada Employment Benefits and Pension Guide (C.C.H.)
- Canadian Advertising and Marketing Law (Young and Fraser; Carswell)
- Canadian Charter of Rights Annotated (Canada Law Book)
- Canadian Charter of Rights Prosecution and Defence of Criminal and Other Statutory Offences (McLeod, Takach, Morton and Segal; Carswell)
- Canadian Commercial Law Guide (C.C.H.)
- Canadian Corporation Precedents (Davies; Carswell)
- Canadian Criminal Code Offences (Gibson; Carswell)
- Canadian Criminal Evidence (McWilliams; Canada Law Book)
- Canadian Divorce Law and Practice (Second Ed.) (MacDonald and Ferrier; Carswell)
- Canadian Employment Benefits and Pension Guide (C.C.H.)
- Canadian Employment Law Guide (C.C.H.)
- Canadian Environmental Law (Butterworths)
- Canadian Estate Planning and Administration Reporter (C.C.H.)
- Canadian Financial Institutions (C.C.H.)
- Canadian Goods & Services Tax Reporter (C.C.H.)
- Canadian Health Case Law Digest (Marshall and Nakatsu; Butterworths)
- Canadian Income Tax (Butterworths)
- Canadian Income Tax Act, Regulations & Rulings (C.C.H.)
- Canadian Industrial Incentives Legislation (Solomon and Cashell; Butterworths)
- Canadian Labour Law Reporter (C.C.H.)
- Canadian Law of Landlord and Tenant (Williams and Rhodes;

Carswell)
- Canadian Law of Planning and Zoning (Rogers; Carswell)
- Canadian Master Tax Guide Updater (C.C.H.)
- Canadian Oil & Gas (Butterworths)
- Canadian Parliamentary Digest (Carswell)
- Canadian Prison Law (Conroy; Butterworths)
- Canadian Real Estate Income Tax Guide (C.C.H.)
- Canadian Sales and Credit Law Guide (C.C.H.)
- Canadian Sales Tax Reporter (C.C.H.)
- Canadian Securities Law Precedents (Davies, Ward and Beck; Carswell)
- Canadian Securities Law Reporter (C.C.H.)
- Canadian Sentencing Digest (Nadin-Davis and Sproule; Carswell)
- Canadian Tax Reporter (C.C.H.)
- Canadian Trade Law Reporter (C.C.H.)
- Canadian Trade-Marks Act — Annotated (Richard; Carswell)
- Carswell's Matrimonial Quantum and Custody Award Service (Carswell)
- Charter of Rights in Litigation (Stratas; Canada Law Book)
- Child Custody Law and Practice (McLeod; Carswell)
- Child Protection Law in Canada (Bernstein, Paulseth, Ratcliffe and Scarcella; Carswell)
- Civil Evidence Handbook (Cudmore; Carswell)
- Cohabitation; The Law in Canada (Holland and Stalbecker-Pountney; Carswell)
- Commercial Crime in Canada (Henderson; Carswell)
- Competition Law Service (Addy and Vanveen; Canada Law Book)
- Computer Law (Sorkman; Carswell)
- Condominium Law and Administration (Loeb; Carswell)
- Construction Builders' and Mechanics' Liens in Canada (Macklem and Bristow; Carswell)
- Counsel Edition, Martin's Criminal Code (Canada Law Book)
- Crankshaw's Criminal Code of Canada (Rodrigues; Carswell)
- Criminal Code Driving Offences (McLeod, Takach and Segal; Carswell)
- Criminal Law Evidence, Practice and Procedure (Gibson; Carswell)
- Criminal Law Precedents (Watt; Carswell)
- Criminal Pleadings & Practice in Canada (Ewaschuk; Canada Law Book)
- Criminal Procedure (Atrens, Burns and Taylor; Butterworths)
- Damages for Breach of Contract (Pitch and Snyder; Carswell)
- Damages for Personal Injury and Death (Goldsmith; Carswell)
- Defence Lawyers Trial Book (Melnitzer, Dawson and Bentley; Butterworths)
- Discrimination and the Law (Tarnopolsky; Carswell)
- Division of Pensions (Pask and Hass; Carswell)

- Dominion Companies Law Reporter (C.C.H.)
- Dominion Tax Cases (C.C.H.)
- Employment Law Manual (Sproat; Carswell)
- Enforcement of Family Law Orders and Agreements: Law and Practice (Wilton and Miyauchi; Carswell)
- Environmental Approvals in Canada (Jeffrey; Butterworths)
- Estate Administration: A Solicitor's Reference Manual (Armstrong; Carswell)
- Evidence and Procedure in Canadian Labour Arbitration (Gorsky, Usprich and Brandt; Carswell)
- Family Law Act of Ontario (Revised Ed.) (MacDonald, Weiler, Mesbur, Perkins and Wilton) (Carswell)
- Federal Limitation Periods (Butterworths)
- Fiduciary Duties in Canada (Ellis; Carswell)
- Free Trade Law Reporter (C.C.H.)
- Freedom of Information (Dombek and Riley; Butterworths)
- Goldsmith on Canadian Building Contracts (Goldsmith and Heintzman; Carswell)
- Government Information: Access and Privacy (McNairn and Woodbury; Carswell)
- Holmested and Watson, Ontario Civil Procedure (Watson and Perkins; Carswell)
- Hughes on Copyright and Industrial Design (Butterworths)
- Hughes on Trade Marks (Butterworths)
- Hughes and Woodley on Patents (Butterworths)
- Income Tax and Family Law Handbook (Rashkis and Benotto; Butterworths)
- International Financial Documentation (Youard; Butterworths)
- Lamont on Real Estate Conveyancing (Carswell)
- Law of Canadian Municipal Corporations (Rogers; Carswell)
- Law of Costs (Orkin; Canada Law Book)
- Law of Damages (Waddams; Canada Law Book)
- Law of Vendor and Purchaser (DiCastri; Carswell)
- Letters of Credit (Sarna; Carswell)
- Limited Partnerships (Hepburn; Carswell)
- Litigation Accounting: The Quantification of Economic Damages (Berenblut and Rosen; Carswell)
- Managing Personal Injury Damages: A Lawyer's Guide (Hollander; Carswell)
- Manes Organized Advocacy (Manes and Edwards; Carswell)
- Manitoba & Saskatchewan Tax Reporter (C.C.H.)
- Manual of Motor Vehicle Law (Third Ed.) (Segal; Carswell)
- Maritimes Tax Reporter (C.C.H.)

- Marriott and Dunn: Practice in Mortgage Remedies in Ontario (Dunn and Gray; Carswell)
- Matrimonial Property Law in Canada (Bissett-Johnson and Holland; Carswell)
- Native Law (Woodward; Carswell)
- New Brunswick Court Forms (Godin and Rouse; Carswell)
- New Brunswick Statute Citator (Carswell)
- New Law of Expropriation (Coates and Waque; Carswell)
- Nova Scotia Annotated Rules of Practice (Ehrlich; Carswell)
- Nova Scotia Statute Citator
- Ontario Corporation Manual (Carswell)
- Ontario Environmental Protection Act Annotated (Saxe; Canada Law Book)
- Ontario Legislative Digest Service (Carswell)
- Ontario Limitation Periods (Butterworths)
- Ontario Regulations Service (Carswell)
- Ontario Tax Reporter (C.C.H.)
- Ontario Taxation Service (Carswell)
- Organized Advocacy A Manual for the Litigation Practitioner (Manes; Carswell)
- Payne's Divorce and Family Law Digest (Carswell)
- Practice and Procedure Before Administrative Tribunals (Macauly; Carswell)
- Property Valuation and Income Tax Implications of Marital Dissolution (Cole and Freedman; Carswell)
- Provincial Inheritance & Gift Tax Reporter (C.C.H.)
- Provincial Succession Duty and Gift Tax Service (Carswell)
- Provincial Taxation Service (Carswell)
- Registration of Title to Land (DiCastri; Carswell)
- Revenue Canada Round Table Annotated (C.C.H.)
- Reville's Divorce Act Annotated (Hainsworth; Canada Law Book)
- Search and Seizure Law in Canada (Hutchison and Morton; Carswell)
- Secured Transactions in Personal Property in Canada (McLaren and deJong; Carswell)
- Securities Law and Practice (Alboini; Carswell)
- Shareholder Remedies in Canada (Peterson; Butterworths)
- Snow's Annotated Criminal Code (Heather; Carswell)
- Tax Planned Will Precedents (Scott-Harston and Johnson; Carswell)
- Transportation Law (Fernandes; Carswell)
- Visual Evidence: A Practitioner's Manual (Goldstein; Carswell)
- Ward's Tax Law and Planning (Davies, Ward & Beck, and Arnold; Carswell)
- Will Precedents, A Solicitor's Manual (Histrop and Cappon; Carswell)

- Williston and Rolls Court Forms (Butterworths)
- Witnesses (Mewett; Carswell)
- Wrongful Dismissal (Harris; Carswell)
- Wrongful Dismissal Practice Manual (Mole; Butterworths)
- Young Offenders Service (Bala and Lilles; Butterworths)

CANADIAN PERIODICALS

- Acta Criminologica (Acta Crim.)
- Actualités (Actualites)
- Administrative Law Journal (Admin. L.J.)
- Advocate/Vancouver Bar Association (Advocate (Van.))
- Advocates' Quarterly (Advocates' Q.)
- Advocates' Society Journal (Advocates' Soc. J.)
- Alberta Law Review (Alta. L.R.)
- Annales du notariat et de l'enregistrement (A. du N.)
- Annals of Air and Space Law (Ann. Air & Sp. L.)
- Annuaire canadien de droit international (A.C.D.I.)
- Assurances (Assurances)
- British Columbia Law Notes (B.C.L.N.)
- Business and the Law (Bus. & L.)
- Business Quarterly (Bus. Q.)
- Cahiers de droit (C. de D.)
- Canadian-American Law Journal (Can.-Am. L.J.)
- Canada-United States Law Journal (Can.-U.S. L.J.)
- Canadian Bar Association Papers (C.B.A. Papers)
- Canadian Bar Association Year Book (C.B.A.Y.B.)
- Canadian Bar Association, British Columbia Branch Lectures (B.C. Br. Lect.)
- Canadian Bar Journal (Can. Bar J.)
- Canadian Bar Review (Can. Bar Rev.)
- Canadian Business Law Journal (Can. Bus. L.J.)
- Canadian Computer Law Reporter (C.C.L.R.)
- Canadian Communications Law Review (Can. Communic. L. Rev.)
- Canadian Community Law Journal (Can. Community L.J.)
- Canadian Criminology Forum (Can. Crim. Forum)
- Canadian Current Tax (Can. Curr. Tax)
- Canadian Council on International Law, Proceedings (Can. Council Int'l L. Proc.)
- Canadian Environmental Law News (Can. Env. L.N.)
- Canadian Human Rights Yearbook (Can. Hum. Rts. Y.B.)
- Canadian Intellectual Property Review (Can. Intell. Prop. Rev.)
- Canadian Journal of Criminology (Can. J. Crim.)

- Canadian Journal of Criminology and Corrections (Can. Crim. & Corr.)
- Canadian Journal of Family Law (Can. J. Fam. L.)
- Canadian Journal of Insurance Law (Can. J. Ins. L.)
- Canadian Lawyer (Can. Law.)
- Canadian Legal Studies (Can. Legal Stud.)
- Canadian Municipal Journal (Can. Mun. J.)
- Canadian Taxation: A Journal of Tax Policy (Can. Tax'n: J. Tax Pol'y)
- Canadian Tax Foundation (Conference Report) (Can. Tax Found.)
- Canadian Tax Journal (Can. Tax J.)
- Canadian Tax News (Can. Tax N.)
- Canadian Year Book of International Law (Can. Y.B. Int'l L.)
- Chitty's Law Journal (Chitty's L.J.)
- Computer Law (Computer L.)
- Corporate Management Tax Conference (Corp. Mgt. Tax Conf.)
- Criminal Law Quarterly (Crim. L.Q.)
- Criminologie (Criminologie)
- Crown Counsel's Review (Crown Coun. Rev.)
- Current Legal Problems (Curr. Legal Probs.)
- Dalhousie Law Journal (Dalhousie L.J.)
- Estates and Trusts Quarterly (Est. & Tr. Q.)
- Family Law Review (Fam. L.R.)
- Gazette/Law Society of Upper Canada (Gazette)
- Health Law in Canada (Health L. Can.)
- Industrial Law Journal (Indust. L.J.)
- Intellectual Property Journal (I.P.J.)
- Journal of Business Law (J. Bus. L.)
- Journal of Law and Social Policy (J.L. & Soc. Pol.)
- Journal of Planning and Environmental Law (J. Plan. & Env. L.)
- Journal of Social Welfare Law (J. Social Welfare L.)
- Law Librarian (L. Lib.)
- Law Quarterly Review (L.Q. Rev.)
- Lawyers Weekly (Lawyers Wkly.)
- Legal Alert (Legal Alert)
- Manitoba Bar News (Man. Bar N.)
- Manitoba Law Journal (Man. L.J.)
- McGill Law Journal (McGill L.J.)
- Modern Law Review (Mod. L. Rev.)
- National Banking Law Review (Nat'l Banking L. Rev.)
- National Insolvency Review (Nat'l Insolv. Rev.)
- Osgoode Hall Law Journal (Osgoode Hall L.J.)
- Ottawa Law Review (Ottawa L. Rev.)
- Provincial Judges Journal (Prov. Judges J.)
- Queen's Law Journal (Queen's L.J.)

- Revue critique de legislation et de jurisprudence du Canada (R.C.L.J.)
- Revue de droit, Université de Sherbrooke (R.D.U.S.)
- Revue de droit de McGill (R.D. McGill)
- Revue de droit du travail (R.D.T.)
- Revue de droit judiciaire (R.D.J.)
- Revue de jurisprudence (R. de J.)
- Revue du Barreau (R. du B.)
- Revue du Barreau canadian (R. du B. can.)
- Revue du Notariat (R. du N.)
- Revue générale de droit (R.G.D.)
- Revue juridique Thémis (R.J. T.)
- Revue legale (R.L.)
- Revue québécoise de droit international (R.Q.D.I.)
- Saskatchewan Bar Review (Sask. Bar. Rev.)
- Saskatchewan Law Review (Sask. L. Rev.)
- Special Lectures of the Law Society of Upper Canada (Spec. Lect. L.S.U.C.)
- Studia Canonica (Stud. Canon.)
- Supreme Court Law Review (Sup. Ct. L. Rev.)
- Uniform Law Conference of Canada, Proceedings (Unif. L. Conf. Proc.)
- University of British Columbia Law Review (U.B.C.L. Rev.)
- University of New Brunswick Law Journal (U.N.B.L.J.)
- University of Toronto Faculty of Law Review (U.T.Fac.L.Rev.)
- University of Toronto Law Journal (U.T.L.J.)
- University of Western Ontario Law Review (U.W.0L. Rev.)
- Windsor Yearbook of Access to justice (Windsor Y.B. Access Just.)

AMERICAN REPORTS

Canadian Law libraries do not generally possess a complete series of all the American State Reports. Most, however, subscribe to the National Reporter System published by the West Publishing Company. This has several series, of which the following are the most important.

- Atlantic Reporter (A.)
- California Reporter (Cal. Rptr.)
- Federal Reporter (F.)
- Federal Rules Decisions (F.R.D.)
- Federal Supplement (F. Supp.)
- New York Supplement (N.Y.S.)
- Northeastern Reporter (N.E.)
- Northwestern Reporter (N.W.)
- Pacific Reporter (P.)

- Southeastern Reporter (S.E.)
- Southern Reporter (So.)
- Southwestern Reporter (S.W)
- Supreme Court Reporter (Sup. Ct.)

The official reports of the U.S. Supreme Court are published in a series cited as U. S. and the reports of the State supreme courts are published in a series referred to by abbreviations of the names of the States, *e.g.*, Mich., N.Y., *etc.* There is a series of annotated reports called the American Law Reports (A.L.R.). Shepard's Citator lists subsequent references to reported cases.

AMERICAN DIGESTS AND ENCYCLOPEDIAS

- American Digest System (Am. Dig.)
- Corpus Juris Secundum (C.J.S.)

Appendix D

CANADIAN COMMON LAW
LAW SCHOOLS

The figures indicate the approximate number of undergraduate students, full-time faculty, and part-time faculty in each school, according to the 1991-92 Directory of the Canadian Association of Law Teachers.

	Students	Full-Time Faculty	Part-Time Faculty
University of Victoria P. 0. Box 2400 Victoria, British Columbia V8W 3H7	300	24	7
University of British Columbia 1822 East Mall Vancouver, British Columbia V6T 1Y1	720	52	67
University of Alberta Edmonton, Alberta T6G 2H5	550	33	38
University of Calgary Calgary, Alberta T2N 1N4	215	19	3
University of Saskatchewan Saskatoon, Saskatchewan S7N OWO	310	27	13
University of Manitoba Winnipeg, Manitoba R3T 2N2	296	24	38

University of Windsor Windsor, Ontario N9B 3P4	420	30	18
University of Western Ontario London, Ontario N6A 3K7	450	31	24
Osgoode Hall Law School York University North York, Ontario M3J 1P3	1021	53	62
University of Toronto Toronto, Ontario M5S 2C5	500	54	61
Queen's University Kingston, Ontario K7L 3N6	475	42	15
University of Ottawa Common Law Section Ottawa, Ontario KIN 6N5	550	36	68

Note: A common law programme is offered both in the French language and the English language. There is also a separate Civil Law Section.

McGill University 3644 Peel St. Montreal, Quebec H3A 1W9	519	45	37

Note: The common law programme is in addition to and overlaps to some extent the traditional Civil Law programme.

University of New Brunswick Fredericton, New Brunswick E3B 5A3	240	19	6
University of Moncton Moncton, New Brunswick E1A 3E9	115	13	10

Note: The programme is in the common law but in the French language.

Dalhousie University Halifax, Nova Scotia B3H 4H9	457	40	44

Appendix E

STATEMENT OF THE ASSOCIATION OF AMERICAN LAW SCHOOLS POLICY ON PRELEGAL EDUCATION

Law schools are necessarily vitally concerned with the quality of the preparation which students entering upon the study of law bring with them from their undergraduate experiences. For unless that preparation has been of high quality, the law schools cannot, in the additional time which they can fairly require of their students, equip them for satisfactory performance within the legal profession and the democratic community.

OBJECTIVES OF PRELEGAL EDUCATION

But while it considers the prescription of particular courses unwise, the association can properly call attention to the quality of undergraduate instruction which it believes fundamental to the later attainment of legal competence. That quality of education is concerned with the development in prelaw students of basic skills and insights. It thus involves education for:

A. Comprehension and expression in words;
B. Critical understanding of the human institutions and values with which the law deals; and
C. Creative power in thinking.

The development of these fundamental capacities is not the monopoly of any subject-matter area, department or division.

Rather, their development is the result of a highly individualized process pursued with high purpose and intensive intellectual effort by persons with at least a reasonable degree of native intelligence. Perhaps the most important variable ingredient of proper climate for this process is the quality of undergraduate instruction. Certainly it is not any particular course or combination of courses. Shortly stated, what the law schools seek in their entering students is not accomplishment in mere memorization but accomplishment in understanding, the capacity to think for themselves and the ability to express their thoughts with clarity and force.

RECOMMENDED LAW PROGRAM

A. *Education for Comprehension and Expression in Words*

The purpose here is to gain both perception and skill in the English language. Language is the lawyer's working tool. He must be able, in the drafting of legal documents, to convey meaning clearly and effectively. In oral and written advocacy he must be capable of communicating ideas convincingly and concisely. In reception no less than in expression, language is fundamental as the lawyer's medium of communication. For the lawyer must be able to grasp the exact meaning of factual statements and legal instruments, to catch the fine points of legal reasoning and argument, and to comprehend the technical materials which constitute the body of the law. To acquire sufficient capacity for communication calls for extensive practice in all phases of the art. Truly, the law trained man, if he is to perform effectively the tasks expected of him, must be a precisionist in the use of language.

What is needed, therefore, is the skill which can be obtained only through practice in:

1. Expression: adequate vocabulary, familiarity with modern usage, grammatical correctness, organized presentation, conciseness and clarity of statement in writing and speaking.
2. Comprehension: concentration and effective recollection in reading and listening, perception of meaning conveyed by verbal symbols.

Both expression and comprehension also require a developed sensitivity to:

3. Fluidity of language: varying meanings of words in different times and contexts, shades of meaning, interpretive problems, hazards in use of ambiguous terms.
4. Deceptiveness of language: emotionally charged words, catch-phrases, hidden meanings of words, empty generalizations.

B. *Education for Critical Understanding of Human Institutions and Values*

The purpose here is to develop insight into, rather than merely information about, the institutions and values with which man is concerned.

One pursuing a legal career encounters all sorts of these institutions under circumstances in which his conduct necessarily shapes the conduct of others in their value choices. Examples are: marriage and the conduct of parties to it; business and the actions of sellers and buyers, stockholders and directors, employers and employees; government and individuals concerned with or subject to taxation, regulation of trade practices, and development of atomic energy; private property and its protection and utilization. It is vital that he performs his work with a consciousness that his conduct counts in the choice of preferable means and ends. This insight comes from intensive study for a substantial period of such of the following areas as he may feasibly undertake, rather than from attempts to skim all the large areas listed. "Study" includes dealing with people in these contexts and reflecting upon the experience thus gained.

Important to the gaining of this insight would be a grasp of:

1. The nature of man and the typical world of which he is a part: stimuli which move him to action, internal and external limitations upon the development of understanding and reason, man's ability to plan conduct and the function of value choices in his planning.
2. The economic systems of societies; theoretical foundations, imperfections in practice, business patterns, the function of governmental processes in economic control.
3. The political organizations of societies: basic theories, modern complexities, the relation of politics to law.
4. The democratic processes in Western societies, especially: responsiveness of governmental policy to popular will, art of compromise, role of education and discussion, functions of majorities and minorities, methods of reconciling competing interests, requirements for participating effectively in world society, degree of efficiency self-government permits, awareness of the moral values inherent in these processes.
5. The social structures of societies: functions of individuals and groups such as the family and churches, implications of the service state, governmental processes in social control, control of the atypical person.
6. The cultural heritages of western societies, including philosophy and ethics; freedom for the individual; traditions of humility, brotherhood and service; inevitability of change and the art of peaceful, orderly adaptation to change.

C. Education for Creative Power in Thinking

The purpose here is to develop the power to think clearly, carefully, and independently. A large part of the work the law-trained person is called upon to do calls for problem solving and sound judgment. This is true regardless of whether he devotes his life to the practice of law, to governmental administration, or to being a judge, legislator, teacher or scholar, or some other endeavour. He will be called upon to create or give advice concerning an almost infinite number of relations. These relationships may range from a comparatively simple contract between a buyer and seller of goods through tailoring a highly complex corporate structure to the needs of a business or nonprofit organization. Any task to which he will be called can be done better if he possesses the power of creative thinking. Predicting the outcome of even routine litigation may involve considering whether a hitherto well-settled rule of law which is applicable would, in the light of the particular facts of the case, possibly be modified or reshaped to avoid unfairness and practical inconvenience. Here the power to think creatively will often merge with critical understanding of human institutions and values, with the latter serving as the necessary threshold to creative power.

Creative power in thinking requires the development of skill in:

1. Research: awareness of sources and types of material, adaptation to particular use, methods of fact presentation.
2. Fact completeness: willingness to recognize all facts, avoidance of preconception and fiction masquerading as fact, disciplined ability to withhold judgments until all the facts are "in".
3. Fact differentiation: relevance of facts to particular issues, varying importance of different facts, relative persuasiveness of various facts.
4. Fact marshalling: reduction of masses of fact to manageable proportions, arrangement of facts in logical and convincing order.
5. Deductive reasoning: use of the syllogism, spotting logical fallacies, avoiding conclusions flowing from inaccurate premises.
6. Inductive reasoning: experimental methodology, accuracy of observation, elimination of variables, role of hypotheses, conditions essential to valid generalization such as adequacy of sampling, strict limitation of conclusions by available reliable data.
7. Reasoning by analogy: methods of classification, gradations of relationship, finding resemblances which justify inferences of similarity.
8. Critical analysis: disciplined skepticism in approach, thoroughness of inquiry, keenness of mind in cutting through to essentials.
9. Constructive synthesis: systematic formulation of principles, meaningful organization of ideas, structural relationships of concepts.
10. Power of decision: resolution of discoverable issues in the light of short- and long-term ends found preferable on explicitly identified and justified grounds.

With the foregoing in mind, the application of the above objectives and a recommended prelegal program in the light of their controlling principles and limitations can be suggested briefly. A particular undergraduate student's reasoning processes may better be developed at a particular institution, for example, by work with a specified teacher of biology than with another teacher of logic, his understanding of cultural heritages may be deepened more by some available courses in literature than by ones open to him in religion, his facility in comprehension and expression in language conceivably strengthened as much or more by work with a history teacher as by some studies in speech or English composition, and his capacity for the handling of facts increased as well by the study of zoology as by the study of sociology, all according to the circumstances obtaining at the particular college and the background of the individual student. In sum, the program of prelegal education which is here earnestly suggested is to be secured through such courses and other work as the student's vital interest, his counselor's judgment as to the quality of instruction, and the facilities of the particular undergraduate school or college dictate in each individual case, considering the development of the student at the time relevant decisions as to his prelegal program are to be carried out.

LIST OF COMMON ABBREVIATIONS

[Note: The English nominate reporters, e.g., A. & E. (Adolphus & Ellis), B. & Ad. (Barnewall & Adolphus) are not included in this list. See above, p. 155. Obvious abbreviations of university law journals are omitted. A complete list can be found in the Index to Legal Periodicals. The abbreviations given in this list are not always the "approved" abbreviations. The list is primarily for readers, not writers.]

A

A., Atlantic Reporter (see above, p. 167)
A.B.A.J., American Bar Association Journal
A.C., Appeal Cases (see above, p. 156)
A.C.J., Associate Chief justice
A.C.W.S., All-Canada Weekly Summaries
A.D.I.L., Annual Digest of International Law
Adjud., Adjudicator
Adm. & Ecc., Admiralty & Ecclesiastical (see above, p. 155)
Admin., Administrator
A.G., Attorney General
Ala. L. Rev., Alabama Law Review
A.L.I., American Law Institute
A. L.J., Australian Law Journal
All E.R., All England Law Reports
All. N.B., Allen's Reports, New Brunswick
A.L.R., American Law Reports
A.L.T., Australian Law Times
Alta. L.R., Alberta Law Reports
Am. Crim. L. Rev., American Criminal Law Review

Am. Dec., American Decisions
Am. Dig., American Digest
Am. J. Comp. L., American Journal of Comparative Law
Am. J. Int. L., American Journal of International Law
Am. J. Legal History, American Journal of Legal History
Anon., Anonymous
App., Appeal
App. Cas., Appeal Cases (see above, p. 156)
App. Div., Appellate or Appeal Division
A.R., Appeal Reports (Ontario), Alberta Reports
Arb., Arbitrator
Arb. Bd., Arbitration Bd.
Arg. L.R., Argus Law Reports (Australia)
Assess., Assessment
Assess. O., Assessment Officer
A.T.D., Australian Tax Decisions
A.T.L.A.J., American Trial Lawyers' Association Journal
Aust. Jur., Australian Jurist

B

B., Baron
Bac. Abr., Bacon's Abridgment
B.C.L.R., British Columbia Law Reports
B.C.R., British Columbia Reports
Bd., Board
B.J. Crim., British Journal of Criminology
B.L.R., Business Law Reports
B.N.A. Act, British North America Act
B.O.D., Butterworths' Ontario Digest
B.R., Banc du roi, banc de la reine (Quebec)
B.T.R., British Tax Review
B.U.L. Rev., Boston University Law Review
Bus. Law., Business Lawyer, The
B.W.C.C., Butterworths' Workmen's Compensation Cases
B.Y.B.I.L., British Year Book of International Law

C

C., Chancellor
C.A., Court of Appeal/Cour d'Appel (Quebec)
Cal. Rptr., California Reporter (see above, p. 167)
Camb. L.J., Cambridge Law Journal
Can. B.A.J., Canadian Bar Association Journal

Can. Bar Rev., Canadian Bar Review
Can. W.L. S., Canadian Weekly Law Sheet
C.A.R., Criminal Appeal Reports
Case W. Res. L. Rev., Case Western Reserve Law Review
C.B., Chief Baron
C.B., Common Bench (reported in English Reports)
C.B.L.J., Canadian Business Law Journal
C.B.R., Canadian Bankruptcy Reports
C.C., Code Civil (Quebec)
C.C., Commercial Cases
C.C.A., Court of Criminal Appeal/Circuit Court of Appeals
C.C.C., Canadian Criminal Cases
C.C.H., Commerce Clearing House
C.C.L., Canadian Current Law
C.C.L.T., Canadian Cases on the Law of Torts
C.C.R., Crown Cases Reserved
C.E.D., Canadian Encyclopedic Digest
C.F. (Appel), Cour fédérale du Canada — Cour d'appel
C.F. (1re inst.), Cour fédérale du Canada — Division de première instance
Ch., Chancery
Ch. Ch., Chancery Chambers Reports (Ontario)
Ch. D., Chancery Division (see above, p. 156)
Chip., Chipman's Reports (New Brunswick)
Chitty L.J., Chitty's Law Journal
Ch. R., Chambers Reports (Ontario)
   Cie, Compagnie
C.J., Chief Justice
C.J.S., Corpus Juris Secundum
C.L., Current Law
C.L.J., Cambridge Law Journal/Canada Law Journal
C.L.L.C., Canadian Labour Law Cases
C.L.P., Current Legal Problems
C.L.R., Commonwealth Law Reports (Australia)
C.L.R.B.R., Canadian Labour Relations Board Reports
C.M.H.C., Canada/Central Mortgage & Housing Corporation
Co. Ct., County Court
Co. Inst., Coke's Institutes
Co. Litt., Coke on Littleton
Com. Dig., Comyn's Digest
Com. L.J., Commercial Law Journal
Comm., Commission
Commr., Commissioner
Cox C.C., Cox's Criminal Cases

C.P., Common Pleas (see above, p. 156)
C.P.C., Carswell's Practice Cases
C.P.D., Common Pleas Division (see above, p. 156)
C.P.R., Canadian Patent Reporter
C. Prov., Cour provinciale
C.R., Criminal Reports
Cr. App. R., Criminal Appeal Reports
C.R.C., Canadian Railway Cases
Crim. L.Q., Criminal Law Quarterly
Crim. L.R., Criminal Law Review
C.R.T.C., Canadian Radio-television Telecommunications Commission
C.S. Can., Cour Suprême du Canada
C.S. Qué., Cour supérieure (Québec)
C.S.P. Qué., Court of Sessions of the Peace (Quebec)/Cour des sessions
de la paix (Québec)
Ct., Court
C.T.C., Canadian Tax Cases/Canadian Transport Cases
Ct. Martial App. Ct., Court Martial Appeal Court

D

Dec. Dig., Decennial Digest (U.S.)
Dep., Deputy
Dick. L.R., Dickinson Law Review
Dist., District
Dist. Ct., District Court
Div., Divisional
Div. Ct., Divisional Court
D.J., District Judge
D.L.R., Dominion Law Reports
Draper, Draper's Upper Canada Reports
D.T.C., Dominion Tax Cases

E

E. & A., Ecclesiastical & Admiralty (see above, p. 155)
E.A.L.R., East Africa Law Reports
E. & A.R., Error and Appeal Reports (Ontario)
E.C.B., Expropriations Compensation Board
E.G., Estates Gazette
E.H.R.R., European Human Rights Reporter
E. & I. App., English and Irish Appeals (see above, p. 155)
E.L.R., Eastern Law Reports
Eq., Equity (see above, p. 155)

E.R., English Reports
E.T.R., Estates and Trusts Reports
Ex., Exchequer (see above, p. 155)
Ex. C.R., Exchequer Court Reports (Canada)

F

F., Faculty Decisions (Scotland), Fraser (Scotland)
Fac. L. Rev., Faculty of Law Review (Toronto)
Fam. Ct., Family Court/Provincial Court (Family Division)
F.C., Federal Court (Canada)
F.C.A., Federal Code Annotated (U.S.)
Fed., Federal
Fed. C.A., Federal Court of Canada — Appeal Division
Fed. T.D., Federal Court of Canada — Trial Division
Fitzh., Fitzherbert's Abridgment
F.M.S.R., Federated Malay States Reports
Ford. L. Rev., Fordham Law Review
Fox. Pat. C., Fox's Patent Cases
F.R.D., Federal Rules Decision (see above, p. 167)
F. Supp., Federal Supplement (see above, p. 167)

G

Geo. L.J., Georgetown Law Journal
Glnv., Glanvil
Govt., Government
Gr., Grant's Chancery Reports (Ontario)
Gr. E. & A., Grant's Error and Appeal Reports (Ontario)

H

Harm., Harman's Upper Canada Common Pleas
Harv. Int. L.R., Harvard International Law Review
Harv. J. Legis., Harvard Journal of Legislation
Harv. L.R., Harvard Law Review
H.C., High Court
H.C.J., High Court of Justice
H.L., House of Lords (see above, p. 155)
H.L.C., House of Lords Cases (reported in the English Reports)
H.L.R., Harvard Law Review
H.O., Hearing Officer, Trade Marks
How., Howard's U.S. Supreme Court Reports

I

I.A.C., Immigration Appeal Cases
I.C.C., Interstate Commerce Commission (U.S.)
I.C.J., International Court of Justice
I. C.J. Y. B., International Court of Justice Yearbook
I.C.L.Q., International and Comparative Law Quarterly
I.J., Irish Jurist
I.L.R., Indian Law Reports
I.L.R., Insurance Law Reports
I.R., Irish Reports
I.R.B., Industrial Relations Board
I.R.C., Internal Revenue Code (U.S.)
Ir. L.T., Irish Law Times
Israel L. Rev., Israeli Law Review

J

J., Justice
J.A., Justice of Appeal
J.C., Judicial Committee
JJ., Justices
J. Law & Econ., Journal of Law and Economics
J. Legal Ed., Journal of Legal Education
Jones, Jones Upper Canada Common Pleas Reports
J.P., Justice of the Peace
J. Pub. L., Journal of Public Law
J.S.P.T.L., Journal of the Society of Public Teachers of Law
Juv. Ct., Juvenile Court

K

K.B., King's Bench (see above, p. 156)
K.C., King's Counsel
Kerr, Kerr's New Brunswick Reports
K.I.R., Knight's Industrial Reports

L

L.A.C., Labour Arbitration Cases
L.C., Lord Chancellor
L.C.B., Land Compensation Board
L.C.J., Lord Chief Justice
L.C.J., Lower Canada Jurist
L.C.L.J., Lower Canada Law Journal

L.C.R., Lower Canada Reports
L.G.R., Local Government Reports
L.J., Law Journal (see above, p. 157)
L.J., Lord Justice
Ll. L.R., Lloyd's List Law Reports
Lloyd's Rep., Lloyd's Reports
L.Q.R., Law Quarterly Review
L.R., Law Reports (see above, p. 155)
L.R.A., Lawyers Reports Announced (U.S.)
L.R.B., Labour Relations Board
L.S.G., Law Society Gazette
L.S.U.C., Law Society of Upper Canada
L.T., Law Times Reports

M

Mag., Magistrate
Man. L.J., Manitoba Law Journal
Man. L.R., Manitoba Law Reports
Man. R., Manitoba Reports
M.C., Magistrates Case (see above, p. 157)/Master's Chambers
Melb. U.L.R., Melbourne University Law Review
M.L.R., Modern Law Review
M.N.R., Minister of National Revenue
Mod. L.R., Modern Law Review
M.P.L.R., Municipal and Planning Law Reports
M.P.R., Maritime Provinces Reports
M.R., Master of the Rolls

N

N.B. Eq. R., New Brunswick Equity Reports
N.B.R., New Brunswick Reports
N.E., Northeastern Reporter (see above, p. 167)
Nfld. & P.E.I.R., Newfoundland and Prince Edward Island Reports
Nfld. R., Newfoundland Reports
N.I., Northern Ireland Law Reports
N.L.J., New Law Journal
N.R., National Reporter
N.S., New Series
N.S.L.R., Nova Scotia Law Reports
N.S.R., Nova Scotia Reports
N.S.W.L.R., New South Wales Law Reports
N.W., Northwestern Reporter (see above, p. 167)

N.W.T.R., North West Territories Reports
N.Y.S., New York Supplement (see above, p. 167)
N.Z.L.R., New Zealand Law Reports

O

O.A.R., Ontario Appeal Reports
O.C., Order in Council
O.L.R., Ontario Law Reports
O.L.R.B., Ontario Labour Relations Board
O.M.B., Ontario Municipal Board
Ont. Div. Ct., Ontario Divisional Court
Ont. Gen. Div., Ontario Court, General Division
Ont. H. C., Supreme Court of Ontario, High Court of Justice (including Family Law Division)
Ont. Prov. Ct. (Civ. Div.), Ontario Provincial Court, Civil Division
Ont. S.C., Supreme Court of Ontario (in Bankruptcy)
Ont. W.C.A.T., Ontario Workers' Compensation Appeals Tribunal
Opp. Bd., Opposition Board
O.R., Ontario Reports
O.S., Old series
O.S.C., Ontario Securities Commission
O.W.N., Ontario Weekly Notes
O.W.R., Ontario Weekly Reporter

P

P., Probate (see above, p. 156)/Pacific (see above, p. 167)/President (judicial title)
Pat. App. Bd., Patent Appeal Board
Pat. Commr., Commissioner of Patents
P.C., Privy Council (see above, p. 155)
P.D., Probate Division (see above, p. 156)
P.D.A., Probate Divorce and Admiralty
P. & D., Probate and Divorce (see above, p. 155)
P.E.I.R., Prince Edward Island Reports
P.G., Procureur général
P.L., Public Law
Prob. Ct., Probate Court
Prop. Comp. Bd., Property Compensation Board
Prov. Ct., Provincial Court (Criminal Division)
P.R., Practice Reports (Ontario)
P.S.A.B., Public Service Adjudication Board
P.S.L.R. Adjud., Public Service Labour Relations Act Adjudicator

P.S.L.R.B., Public Service Labour Relations Board
P.S.S.R.B., Public Service Staff Relations Board
P.U.(C.) Bd., Public Utilities (Commissioners') Bd.
Pub. L., Public Law

Q

Q.B., Queen's Bench (see above, p. 156), see also Q.B.R. below
Q.B.R., Queen's Bench Reports (reprinted in English Reports)
Q.C., Queen's Counsel
Q.L.J., Queensland Law Journal
Q.L.R., Quebec Law Reports/Queensland Law Reports
Q.S.R., Queensland State Reports
Que. C.A., Quebec Court of Appeal
Que. L.R.B., Quebec Labour Relations Board (Commission des relations
   de travail du Québec)
Que. Q.B., Quebec Queen's Bench
Que. S.C., Quebec Superior Court
Q.U.L.J., Queensland University Law Journal
Qd. R., Queensland Report

R

R., Regina/Queen/Reine/Rex/King/Roi
R.A.C., Ramsay's Appeal Cases (Canada)
Reg., Registrar
Rev. Leg., Revue Legale
Rev. Stat., Revised Statutes
R.F.L., Reports of Family Law
R.J.O., Rapports Judiciaires Officiels (Quebec)
R.L., Revue Legale
Rob. U.C., Robinson's Reports (Ontario)
R.P.C., Reports of Patent Cases
R.P.R., Real Property Reports
R.R., Revised Reports
R.R.(O.), Revised Regulations (of Ontario)
R.S., Revised Statutes (*e.g.*, R.S.O., Revised Statutes of Ontario)
R.T.P. Comm., Restrictive Trade Practices Commission
R.T.R., Road Traffic Reports

S

S., Session Cases (Scotland), Statutes (*e.g.*, S.C., Statutes of Canada)
S.A.L.J., South African Law Journal

S.A.L.R., South Australian Law Reports/South African Law Reports
Sask. L.R., Saskatchewan Law Reports
S.A.S.R., South Australian State Reports
S.C., Session Cases (Scotland)/Supreme Court
S.C.C., Supreme Court of Canada
Sc. & Div., Scottish and Divorce (see above, p. 155)
Scot. Jur., Scottish Jurist
S.C.R., Supreme Court Reports
S.E., Southeastern Reporter (see above, p. 168)
Sess. Cas., Session Cases (Scotland)
S.F.L.J., San Francisco Law Journal
S.J., Solicitors Journal
S.L.R., Saskatchewan Law Reports, Scottish Law Reports
S.L.T., Scottish Law Times
Sm. L.C., Smith's Leading Cases
So., Southern Reporter (see above, p. 168)
Sol. J., Solicitors Journal
S.P., Sessions of the Peace
S.R., State Reports (New South Wales)
Stat., Statutes (*e.g.*, Stat Can. *or* S.C.)
St. Tr., State Trials
Stu. K.B., Stuart's Lower Canada Reports
Surr. Ct., Surrogate Court
S.W, Southwestern Reporter (see above, p. 168)
Syd. L.R., Sydney Law Review

T

T.A.B.C., Tax Appeal Board Cases
Tas. L.R., Tasmania Law Reports
Tas. U.L.R., Tasmania University Law Review
T.B., Tariff Board
T.C., Tax Cases
T.C.C., Tax Court of Canada
T.D., Supreme Court, Trial Division
Terr. Ct., Territorial Court
Terr. L.R., Territories Law Reports
T.L.R., Times Law Reports
T.O., Taxing Office(r)
T.R.B., Tax Review Board
Trib., Tribunal
Tupp., Tupper's Reports (Ontario)

U

U.C.C., Uniform Commercial Code
U.C.C.C., Uniform Consumer Credit Code
U.C., Ch., Upper Canada Chancery
U.C. Chamb., Upper Canada Chambers
U.C.C.P., Upper Canada Common Pleas
U.C.E. & A., Upper Canada Errors & Appeals
U.C.Jur., Upper Canada Jurist
U.C.K.B., Upper Canada King's Bench
U.C.L.J., Upper Canada Law Journal
U.C.O.S., Upper Canada Oil Series
U.C.P.R., Upper Canada Practice Reports
U.C.Q.B., Upper Canada Queen's Bench
U.F.C., Unified Family Court
U. Tasm. L.R., Tasmania University Law Review
U.T.L.J., University of Toronto Law Journal
U.Tor.L.J., University of Toronto Law Journal
U.W.A.L.R., University of Western Australia Law Review
U.W.O.L.J., University of Western Ontario Law Journal

V

V.C., Vice-Chancellor
V.L.R., Victoria Law Reports (Australia)
V.R., Victoria Reports (Australia)

W

W.A.L.R., Western Australia Law Reports
W.C.B., Workmen's/Workers' Compensation Board
W.C.R., Workmen's Compensation Reports
Whart., Wharton's Reports (Pennsylvania)
Wheat., Wheaton's Reports (U.S.)
W.L.R., Western Law Reporter (Canada), Weekly Law Reports (England)
W.L.T, Western Law Times,
W.N., Weekly Notes
W.R., Weekly Reporter
W.W.R., Western Weekly Reports

INDEX